Family Walks
in
North Worcestershire

Edited by Margaret Cooper

15 walks with maps specially prepared by
the Ramblers Association Bromsgrove Group

hb Halfshire Books

First published in Great Britain in 1991 by
Halfshire Books
6 High Street, Bromsgrove
Worcestershire B61 8HQ

Copyright © 1991 Halfshire Books
ISBN 0 9513525 4 7

Puublishers' note
While every care has been taken in compiling this book the publishers cannot accept responsibility for any inaccuracies. Things change rapid!y: what was correct even a month ago may not be so today. We would be happy to know of any changes you may discover on any of these walks.

Typeset by Wyvern Typesetting, Worcester
Printed in Great Britain by Billing & Sons Ltd.

Contents

Map symbols

Each walk is accompanied by a specially prepared map meant to be used in conjunction with the relevant OS map.

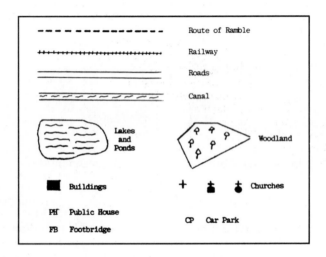

Follow the Country Code

Guard against all risks of fire
Take your litter home
Fasten all gates
Keep to public paths across farmland
Use gates and stiles to cross fences, hedges and walls
Keep dogs under control
Leave livestock, crops and machinery alone
Help to keep all water clean
Take special care on country roads
Make no unnecessary noise
Protect wildlife, plants and trees
Enjoy the countryside and respect its life and work

Introduction

Almost three years ago we published *Family Walks Around Bromsgrove and Droitwich.* It proved instantly popular and has for some time been out of print. We considered reprinting but decided instead to publish an entirely new collection of local walks. Once again, the Ramblers Association Bromsgrove Group responded manfully — and womanfully — choosing, checking and writing up fifteen of its favourite walks in North Worcestershire.

The Group goes from strength to strength: it has a large membership, it organises over twenty-five walks every year and the walks it produced for that first book have clearly given a lot of pleasure to many people.

This new collection covers what is still a pleasantly rural part of the county, despite its proximity to England's second city, and takes the rambler over hills and down dales, through woods and tiny hamlets, across streams, canals and railway lines, past churches, cottages and fine country houses.

To the basic route provided by the local group of the Ramblers Association has been added some brief historical and topographical information which can easily be filled out, for those interested, by a visit to the local library. An outstanding feature of the walks is the number of old houses in the area which serve to remind us of the great religious strife and persecution of the seventeenth century.

Two walks deserve special mention. A ramble over motorway footbridges might at first seem almost a contradiction in terms. It is however a very interesting walk and it is heartening to see how much of the old footpath network has been preserved despite the slicing up of the countryside to accommodate more and more traffic. The Studley — Coughton walk is, of course, cheating. But it is such pleasant walking country and so near to the Worcestershire — Warwickshire border that there was no agonising about its inclusion.

In the introduction to our first book of walks we spoke about the right to responsible roaming. The growing pressure on land use continues to threaten this right but we are confident that a sensible approach by landowners and walkers will secure the spider's web of foot- and bridlepaths. We would like to urge walkers to respect both the owner and the land they enjoy and owners to respond by keeping open long-recognised rights of way and maintaining stiles and openings.

There is nothing new about walking groups. In Worcetershire at least organised rambling has an honourable history. But times and outlooks change and we begin this 1991 collection with an account of a couple of local walks from the more leisurely, yet curiously purposeful, days of the nineteenth century.

Rambling Victorians: seaside orchids in Hanbury, strawberry chaos at Dodford

One fine day in late August 130 years ago a group of gentlemen assembled in Droitwich and proceeded to make their way to Hanbury Hall which the owner, H Foley Vernon Esq, had obligingly thrown open for inspection. They toured the large brick edifice, virtually unchanged since its erection in 1701, admired some of the strikingly beautiful family portraits and cracked a few clever jokes about 'the Straits of Malvern' as they stood gazing at a portrait of George I which showed Worcester Cathedral beside a sea full of ships.

Then they walked up to the church, discussing as they went the remarkable little hill on which it was so inconveniently sited and the origin of its name. *Ambury*, they decided, was undoubtedly what it was first called, a name given to sacred places in heathen Celtic times. Prying about the churchyard they found a most unusual headstone to a parish clerk said to have been an outstanding tenor (though far from upright, the headstone can still be seen). In addition to the inscription there is a line of music — 'I know that my Redeemer liveth' — which, it was generally felt, was not much use to the fellow below.

> Tho' o'er his grave
> Is placed a stave

as the bard of the party put it.

Having stopped to admire the wonderful view they moved off through a dense little wood to the west, coming across the Greater Butterfly Orchid in great numbers, normally only found near the sea; and spent a fascinating time pottering on Dodderhill Common, then in a primitive gorsey state, several of the trees standing out like spectres, leafless through disease and exposure, but home to some rare fungi. Between Hadzor and Hanbury a great quanity of the beautiful crimson Grass Veitch was found and a specimen of the uncommon Natterjack.

By now they were hungry, so they hastened to the Vernon Arms for a late dinner, then strolled to a nearby quarry where they had been told they would find fossils. They were disappointed, however — it was the wrong sort of rock for fossils. Nevertheless, some insisted on looking since the colour on the map they were using suggested there *ought* to be fossils! But evening was coming on, the stubborn ones were rounded up and all returned to Droitwich in carriages.

The men who had enjoyed such an interesting day out were members of the Worcestershire Naturalists' Club, formed in 1847 to study the natural history, geology and ancient remains of the county. Actually they went further afield than that with trips into the surrounding counties and visits to such far-flung spots as Bosworth Field, Abergavenny, Weston-super-Mare and Monmouth — but then there was a very decent rail service in the last century and, failing this, a choice of carriages. They were keen observers and reporters of everything they saw. Their leisurely but purposeful rambles usually appeared in the local press and although they were essentially a field club they also met in the Natural History Room in Foregate Street in Worcester (demolished in 1939) to listen to learned papers, engage in discussion and examine exhibits.

It goes without saying that it was an entirely male preserve, at least for the first fifty years. Not until 1895 were the rules altered to admit lady members — and the first, Emma Rose, was the daughter of the president and soon married to a leading committee member. For half a century, though, it was a men-only group: a great number of clergymen, a good sprinkling of doctors, several businessmen, a few academics and even the odd newspaper editor who was able to leave the presses for a mid-week ramble.

In July 1877 the naturalists assembled in Bromsgrove where they stood in St John's churchyard listening to a paper read by Mr J Noake, while someone went to fetch the key. The paper on the history of the area was far from short but amongst other things it dismissed the idea that Robin Hood had once resided in the district and praised the improvements to the 'grand old parish church' which a quarter of a century before had been so dilapidated.

Noting that an old and shattered yew tree in the churchyard might well be the oldest in Worcestershire the attentive group examined the interior of the church, then crossed the fields to Fockbury Mill and walked along the lanes to Bournheath. There they inspected the *Bumble Hole,* a totally dark cavern in the sandstone rock, once the home of a hermit.

In warm and sultry weather they crossed the valley and reached Dodford where in the opinion of this establishment group 'the noted charlatan Feargus O'Connor tried to establish one of his socialist colonies'. Now, they saw with approval, the allotments laid out by O'Connor were given over to strawberries. And it was probably the vast quanitities of the luscious fruit before them that caused the well-planned ramble to fall apart. Some went off to Alfred's Well, keen to sample the water; some flatly refused to believe the Saxon King had ever been near there and made straight for the Priory; the rest gave both well and priory a miss and stayed behind to feast on the strawberries. The few who listened to the second paper of the day — on the history of Dodford Priory — were disappointed with what they found: a labrynth of 'modern' rooms worked into much less of the original buildings than they had expected.

By this time however the party had got itself together again and pushed on through Randan and Pepper Woods, emerging onto a grassy top from where there were wonderful views of Herefordshire, Shropshire and the Welsh Borders. But they were tired and hungry and relieved to be told that they were close to Fairfield House.

After a substantial lunch they felt much better; but their walking for the day was over for a visit to Bell Hall to inspect the elegant gardens was made by carriage. Their final visit was to Madeley Heath but they found the boulders of the Glacial Period not as gigantic as they had been led to believe and drove rapidly back to Bromsgrove where, just after five, they sat down to dinner at the *Golden Cross*. And finally, at the end of a long day, they made their way back to the station at Aston Fields where early evening trains took them to their various destinations.

The Worcestershire Naturalists' Club lives on. Do its members walk as far? Eat as much? And can they all get home by train?

Harvington

Walk 1   *Hiding holes and bluebells*

4½ miles
Harvington—Mount Segg—Harvington
OS Pathfinder Map   953 (SO 87/97)
Start and finish   Harvington Hall car park (GR 877744)

Harvington is one of several little hamlets in the large parish of Chaddesley Corbett, which takes its name from the main village, an area relying traditionally on agriculture and horticulture but with many of its inhabitants these days working in Birmingham, Bromsgrove and Kidderminster.

The first glimpse of Harvington Hall is marvellous: this beautifully moated house, all gables and chimneys, stands mellow and inviting even in the filthiest weather. It's a must to visit and revisit and there is plenty of interest for the whole family. So allow time at the beginning or end of the walk.

It has been said that Worcestershire is richer in secret hiding places than any other county, most of them connected with the persecution of Catholics. Harvington is one of the most interesting historic houses in the West Midlands and L T C Rolt considered it to be England's finest 'Catholic stronghold'. Sir John Pakington, wealthy lawyer and staunch Protestant (**see** Walk 4), bought the medieval H-plan timber-framed building in the 1530s (he acquired the odd 29 other manor houses in his time—an early collector?); but it was a later family member, Humphrey, who altered and enlarged it and a later one still who converted to Catholicism and equipped the place with a variety of ingenious hiding places.

Here Father Wall made his headquarters, captured accidentally at nearby Rushock Court (they were looking for a debtor — unpaid poll tax, perhaps). He was the last man to be hung for his faith (at Worcester in 1679). Harvington then passed to the Throckmorton family who added some servants' quarters but didn't live in it all that much. Gradually, most of its fixtures and furnishings — even the great staircase — were stripped away and taken to Coughton Court so that at the beginning of this century it presented a woeful sight, a derelict shell, almost beyond repair. Thankfully it was bought by the Catholic Archdiocese of Birmingham in 1923 and restored to its former beauty.

Join the metalled lane, keeping the hall on the left, and go past the big old grey tree stump and past the moat. Continue down the lane until you come to a corner (with a little brick wall on the left). Leave the lane, turning right onto a wide track which leads across the fields. On reaching

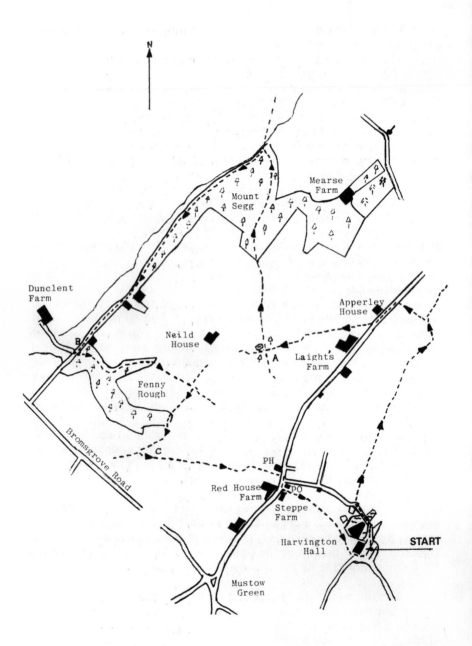

N

Mearse
Farm

Mount
Segg

Dunclent
Farm

Apperley
House

B

Neild
House

A

Laight's
Farm

Fenny
Rough

Bromsgrove Road

C

PH

Red House
Farm

PO

Steppe
Farm

Harvington
Hall

START

Mustow
Green

10

the next corner leave this wide track by bearing left to cross the field, keeping the hedge to the right.

Continue along the edge of the field and at the end of the first field proceed along the edge, following a path that runs alongside a barbed wire fence on the left. Just before you enter the next field you will see a rusty gate, with an old tree stump on your right and an orchard on the left. *Ignore* the small stile at the end of the barbed wire fence and, instead, carry straight ahead alongside a hedge on the left. Turn left at a gap in the hedge, ignoring the stile on your right as you turn through the hedge. Keeping the fence on your right, proceed to the main road (A450)

At the main road cross over and turn left, passing Apperley House ('Pattajohn Dogs for Sale'). In about 30 yards look for a hole in the hedge on your right and, as there is no signpost here, pick up a right of way which goes diagonally across a very large field, passing well behind Laight's Farm. Again, look for a large gap in the hedge. In front of you is a brown water tower raised on four tall metal legs. Head for a large clump of trees in a hollow in the field which hides a pond. Aim to the left of the pond (**A**) and turn sharp right when you reach the trees, making towards the extreme left of the wood.

On reaching a track bear right and, keeping the hedge on the left, proceed along the bridleway, heading towards the wood in front of you. Enter the wood through the small gate and follow the sandy track. The wood you are in is a private nature reserve, owned by the farmer at Dunclent who is only too happy for walkers to take advantage of this ancient right of way. It's a very pretty place with a profusion of bluebells in the spring and sweet chestnuts in the autumn. On Mount Segg there are badgers and in this area you may well spot some of the farmer's many different breeds of wildfowl. At a fork in the track take the righthand track (still sandy) leading through silver birches. The track narrows between ferns and quite soon opens out into a clearing and becomes much wider.

Proceed through the clearing, keeping to the wide sandy track which sweeps left along the outer edge of the wood. Near the end of the wood, just before a small bridge, take the wide path that bears to the left, again following the periphery of the wood. At the end of the wood climb the stile into the lane and take the right fork. After passing the second house (Woodlands), turn into a gateway on your left and bear right to the wood (**B**). Carry on to a stile in the lefthand corner which leads into the wood. Over the stile, proceed straight ahead and quite soon pick up a track which bears to the left between the trees.

Follow this track as it winds upwards to the end of the wood and an open field. The path leads straight across the field, passing underneath the telegraph lines (and keeping Neild House to your left); and then slopes down to a dip by a hedge. Go down a bank into the next field and turn right, heading towards a small wood (Fenny Rough). Follow the narrow path into the wood and cross the small stream, passing a little pumphouse on the left. Climb the stile at the end of the wood.

Ahead you can see the steeple of Stone Church. The right of way leads straight across the field though not many yards across there is a wire fence. Pass under the telegraph lines and turn sharp left (**C**). Aim for the stile in the lefthand corner of the field. (At the time of writing, a low electrified wire had been put halfway across.) Cross the stile, keeping the hedge on your left, and after about 50 yards cross another stile on the left in the hedge.

Go down a bank to a footbridge across a stream, climb the bank the other side and follow the footpath alongside *The Dog*. Climb the stile into the road, cross over and turn right, ignoring the sign to Harvington Hall. Just before Steppe Farm turn left into a metalled drive, keep left into a field and keep the hedge trees to the left. Cross the stile in the left corner of the field and in the next field walk along the pathway, past the ponds on the left. You're now at the back of Harvington Hall with the moat on your left. Follow the track back to the car park.

Walk 2   *Over the ridge*

4½ miles
Alvechurch — Rowney Green — Alvechurch
OS Pathfinder Map   954 (SP 07/17)
Start and finish   Park either in The Square (GR 029726) or in the public carpark behind the *Red Lion* (GR 027727). The Midland Red Bus 148 also stops at The Square.

Lying midway between Redditch and the edge of Birmingham, Alvechurch is a substantial and very interesting village, well worth a leisurely look at the beginning or end of the walk. It is named after the Saxon woman who founded, or owned, its first church, Aelfgyth. Today's parish church, rising above the surrounding houses, stands on the site of that first building, heavily restored in Victorian times but still with its medieval tower.

Before Birmingham and Redditch were even thought of Alvechurch was a borough with its own mayor. In the north-east corner of the village (behind The Moat House) is the site where the bishops of Worcester once had their medieval summer palace. But the Black Death dealt a devastating blow and a bleak little report at the time of the Reformation shows how far things had sunk:

> *Plate none, goods none, preachers none, schools none.*

That it recovered handsomely is obvious to anyone visiting the place. Its buildings range from typical Worcestershire half-timbered houses to cottages of local brick. Wherever you look there's something of interest — the Old Forge, the *Swan Inn*, the Post Office and Old Grammar School, the Old House . . . And several of the mills, once powered by the River Arrow, remain as evidence of the working life of earlier centuries.

Alvechurch is no longer a borough; in the middle of the last century the poor old mayor couldn't afford the cost of the banquet he was required to give. But, more important, the village is now a designated conservation area, a result of concern expressed over the years that if something wasn't done yet another historic village would lose all its character.

Take the main road, walking uphill towards Redditch and passing the *Swan Inn* on the right. After about ¼ mile turn left between two pillars clearly marked 'Lodge Farm'. Walk up the track, crossing the River Arrow, and where the track bends climb a stile on the right and proceed on a well marked-track over Newbourne Hill.

13

14

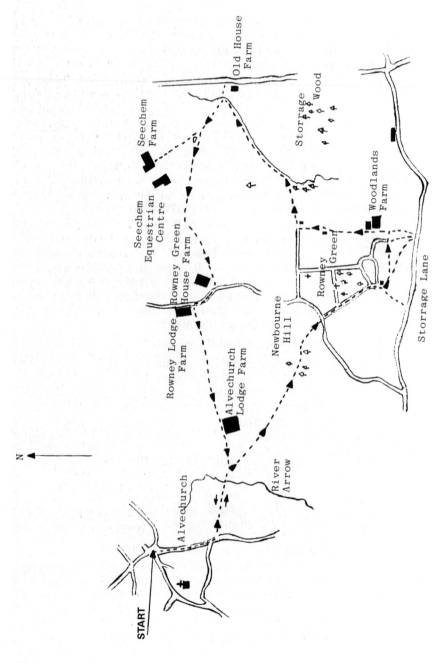

N

START

Alvechurch

River
Arrow

Alvechurch
Lodge Farm

Rowney Lodge
Farm

Rowney Green
House Farm

Seechem
Equestrian
Centre

Seechem
Farm

Old House
Farm

Newbourne
Hill

Rowney Green

Storrage
Wood

Woodlands
Farm

Storrage Lane

At the gate at the top and before climbing the steps turn to look at the view down over Alvechurch and on to Redditch. Then follow the path to Rowney Green, coming out opposite Gravel Pit Lane. Rowney Green straddles a green ridge south-east of Alvechurch. Farming has always been the main occupation but as the name of the lane and a look at the OS map suggest gravel-working has been important too.

Go down Gravel Pit Lane, ignoring a stile on the left, to a cottage at the bottom. Take a footpath to the right of the cottage, go over a footbridge and bear left. Keep to the line of the hedge, pass a stile on the left which looks as if it goes to a cottage, and go through a gate in the lefthand corner of the field. Turn left over a stile and continue over a ditch crossing, passing Woodland Farm on the right. Avoiding the cattle-grid, go to the lefthand side of the hedge and then pick up an old green lane, passing two houses, one on the right, then one on the left.

Where the lane ends at some new stable buildings take the righthand stile and continue downhill to the next stile. Head for the corner of the field to a stream where at the right time of the year there is a good bed of watercress. Use the cattle-crossing to the right of the original brick bridge (now derelict) and cross over the stile opposite. Follow the line of the hedge and stream on the right across two more fields. Ignore the footbridge ahead and turn left where the path meets another path coming from the right.

Continue with the hedge on the left, cross over two more stiles and, keeping the pond on the right, bear left to the corner of the field. Cross a track to the next stile, head towards Rowney Green House Farm, with Seechem Equestrian Centre on the right, climb a stile in a wire fence and go through the gate and along the farm track with the farmhouse on the right.

Old farm names seem to be under threat. Rowney Green House Farm — shown on the map and known locally by that traditional name — is now called Emma Dale Farm. Turn right into the road and a few yards later turn left at a bridleway signpost, just before the farm now renamed Alpine Lodge Farm (on the map still called Rowney Lodge Farm).

A hundred years ago the farmers and labourers at Seechem (just behind Seechem Equestrian Centre and now called Seechem Manor) gathered in the great barn for the time-honoured harvest supper:

At the end of the table sat a huge joint of beef,
a roast goose and a great home-cured ham
which John Yeoman was carving with great
expertise. On the table — Nora feared it might
be in danger of collapsing — was every kind
of vegetable that could be grown in the
Seechem fields, except the common

mangold. When the main course was over an
enormous plum pudding was carried in to the
cheering company; and as if this were not
enough, it was followed by pies and tarts of
every description and an endless supply of
cider to swill it all down.

(From *Seechem Chronicles* by W Eileen Davies, 1990)

On reaching Alvechurch Lodge Farm follow the path to rejoin the original track and turn right at the road and back to the village.

Seechem Manor

Walk 3   *'The squire's' country*

7 miles
Bentley — Hanbury — Stock and Bradley — Bentley
OS Pathfinder Map   974 (SO86/96)
Start and finish   Layby to the east of the T-junction ¼ mile west of
Lower Bentley Farm (or the grass verge opposite)
(GR 975658)

A walk through three parishes — large Hanbury, medium-sized Bentley Pauncefoot and small Stock and Bradley (briefly!) — without coming across anything approaching a centre of population.

The rather aristocratic-sounding Bentley Pauncefoot gets its name from three very down-to-earth elements: two Old English words, *beonet* and *leah*, meaning a clearing which has overgrown with grass or reeds; and the Norman nickname (after Richard Panzeout who held the manor in the twelfth century) meaning 'round belly'.

The Cookes family owned Bentley manor for a couple of hundred years, Sir Thomas rescuing Bromsgrove School in the late seventeenth century by providing the money to refound it. Nearer our time Bentley achieved great fame through its squire, a superb rider and master of the Bentley Harriers, known throughout England and regularly reported in the sporting press. It was acknowledged as excellent hunting country and to the manor house came the cream of sporting society. The squire, incidentally, was a woman, Mrs Maudie Cheape, who inherited the estate (some 140 farms and cottages) in the 1880s — over her brother. Those were the days.

From the layby go back to the T-junction and take the gated track opposite up to the top of the slope and another gate. Through the gate go left and follow the hedgerow through one gate and on to another. Once through this gate cross the field to the stile-and-ditch crossing and then cross the next field to the stile into the lane. Turn right into the lane; walk past the cottage on the left and footpath on the right (which marks the boundary between Bentley Pauncefoot and Hanbury parishes) and go through a gate which leads to a green track.

In a few yards the track turns sharp right and a stile can be seen on the left just past an unusual 'sunrise' metal gate. Leave the track at this stile and bear left down the slope towards a coppice (Ash Plantation). Follow the path through the wood and carry on up the slope towards the track leading to Forest Farm. At the track go through the gate on the left and through the farmyard to the road.

Cross the road to a small gate to the left of a metal one and then enter a long pasture field via another gate. Pass a barn on the left and a

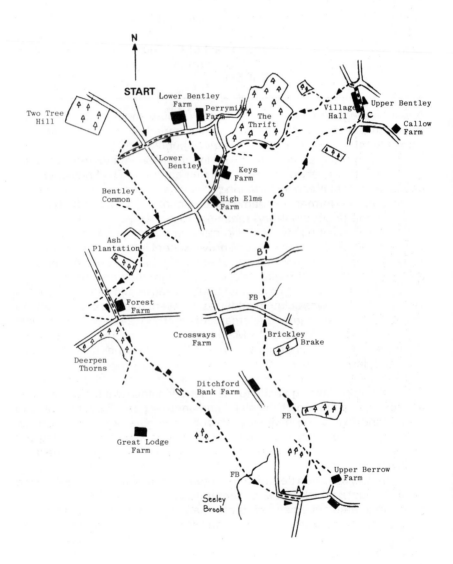

N

START

Two Tree Hill

Lower Bentley Farm

Perrymill Farm

The Thrift

Village Hall

Upper Bentley

Callow Farm

Lower Bentley

Keys Farm

Bentley Common

High Elms Farm

Ash Plantation

B

Forest Farm

FB

Deerpen Thorns

Crossways Farm

Brickley Brake

Ditchford Bank Farm

FB

Great Lodge Farm

FB

Upper Berrow Farm

A

Seeley Brook

pond on the right and continue to the end of the field. Go through two gates and then proceed — with the hedge on the left—up and then down the slope to a gate and a brook. (NB The OS map shows the footpath on the other side of the hedge for the second half of this field but the gate is *definitely* to the right of the hedge.) Cross the brook — into the parish of Stock and Bradley — and follow the hedge on the right to the road (**A**).

At the road bear right for a short distance to the T-junction. Take the lane ahead and immediately go left onto a footpath just past the first fence. Follow the fence to cross a strip of woodland. (To the right is Upper Berrow Farm which takes its name from one of the squire of Bentley's favourite hunting places, Berrow Hill, just to the south-east, a nice little bit of tautology, incidentally, since Berrow means 'hill' anyway). Then go ahead into the next field. As you come to the top of a small rise bear slightly left to a stile and footbridge in the dip to the left of the wood. The brook, Seeley Brook, is the same one crossed earlier and once over you are back in the parish of Hanbury.

Bear slightly left across the next field to a gate into the drive of Ditchford Bank Farm. Take the gate opposite and cross the field to a stile in the hedge. Go under the power cables in the field ahead to a stile onto the road. Cross the road, climb the stile and head across the field to emerge onto a track alongside a cottage on the right (**B**).

Turn right and in front of the cottage go through the first gate on the left and follow the hedge on the right. In the corner of the field carry on, with the hedge on the left, past a pool on the right and on to another stile. Over this stile bear right to the corner of the field and then continue in the next field with the hedge on the left to the corner of the field. Carry on with the hedge now on the right, for a short distance, then go up the slope bearing left at the top to a stile into a rough area. Another stile on the bank to the left of a pool leads to a field. Make towards the buildings ahead and emerge onto a track near a sharp bend in the road (**C**).

Please note It is possible to walk more directly from **B** to **C** by going ahead at the cottage and following the bridlepath all the way. *But* the route is usually very wet and muddy and best attempted only after a spell of dry weather.

At the road bear left past Bentley Village Hall and left at the road junction. Just past the house on the left take the signposted stile into the garden and then out again into the field. Carry on with the hedge on the right to the point where the hedge bears sharp right. Cross the stream and go left down the slope to a hedge; bear right for a few yards to a stile on the left. Over the stile cross two railway sleepers — posing as a bridge — over a ditch and bear slightly right to the edge of the private woods, The Thrift. Turn left and follow the edge of the woods through a series of small gates, crossing a field to emerge at a road with a triple signpost.

Turn left along the road past Britannia House (on the right) and after 200 yards take a signposted footpath on the right. Bear right across the field to a stile almost in the corner. Over this stile bear left across the corner of the field to another stile. Continue straight ahead across the next field to a stile and then straight on to the last stile-and-ditch crossing into the lane. Turn left for the ¼-mile walk back to the starting point.

Bradley Green Church — a timely warning

Walk 4 *Green fields*
7 miles
Cutnall Green — **Hampton Lovett** — **Elmbridge** — **Cutnall Green**
OS Pathfinder Map 974 (SO 86/96)
Start and finish *The Live and Let Live* on the A422, Cutnall Green
(Obtain the landlady's permission) (GR 880685)

This walk is a fairly gentle one through the parishes of Hampton Lovett and Elmbridge, a chance to appreciate some pleasant and peaceful farming country in the area north of Droitwich. Those prepared to make a couple of short diversions will be rewarded by the sight of two very attractive village churches.

One hundred and fifty years ago George Griffiths — who was conducting a one-man campaign against badly managed schools — described Cutnall Green as *'a quiet road-side place, remarkable only for breeding geese, for a very badly managed school, and very bad annual races* (behind The Chequers)'. Today's village school would be very much more to his liking and the races have long gone. Now it is probably best known for the good food available from *The Live and Let Live*. But some things don't change. Apart from the traffic at certain times of the day it is still a quiet roadside place - and the geese are holding their own. You'll probably hear them as you set out since they live next door but two to the pub.

Out of the pub car park turn left onto the main road and left again in 50 yards onto a footpath to New Road. The path is very narrow and in places very overgrown. Cross the road and go through a kissing gate and across a playing field. To the right can be seen the back of the village school George Griffiths would approve of; and ahead in the distance is Abberley Hill. Keep to the lefthand hedge, go over the stile and proceed along the righthand hedgeside to a footbridge at the bottom of the field. From this field you can see the spire of Elmley Lovett Church to the right.

(*Note* If there are bulls in the field return to New Road, turn right and walk down to the crossroads* where the walk can be picked up again)

After the footbridge walk almost due west across an arable field to a gate and stile on the lefthand side. Climb the stile and follow the lefthand hedgeside heading south. Go over the next stile and, still keeping south, cross the field to reach the stile in the hedge on the roadside.

Turn left towards the crossroads (200 yards). *This is where the walk can be picked up again if the bulls prove troublesome. At the crossroads turn right (signposted Doverdale) and walk under the railway

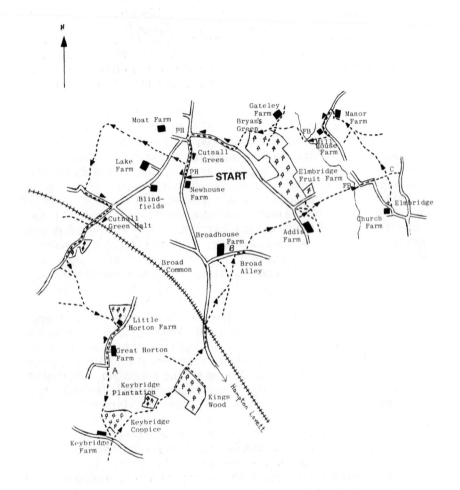

N

Moat Farm

PH

Gateley
Farm

Bryan's
Green

Manor
Farm

FB

Cutnall
Green

Hill
House
Farm

Lake
Farm

PH

START

Elmbridge
Fruit Farm

C

Blind-
fields

Newhouse
Farm

FB

Elmbridge

Cutnall
Green Halt

Church
Farm

Broadhouse
Farm

Addis
Farm

Broad
Common

Broad
Alley

Little
Horton Farm

Great Horton
Farm

A

Keybridge
Plantation

Kings
Wood

Hampton Lovett

Keybridge
Coppice

Keybridge
Farm

bridge, passing woods on the left and coming to a stile by a gate on the lefthand side at the end of the woods (about 500 yards from the railway bridge).

Cross the field to a gate directly opposite the stile. Walk the length of the field to the far end where there are three oak trees and take the lefthand one of a pair of gates (between two of the oak trees). NB — only Superman can open this gate easily. The trick, if you don't already know, is to stand on the bottom rung - then it's simple! In the next field walk in an easterly direction following the hedgerow on the left to Little Horton Farm (a timber yard). Cross over the stile between the barn and the house onto the lane and turn right.

Walk along the lane past Great Horton Farm on the left (Horton, incidentally — or *hor, tun* in the Domesday Book — means 'muddy farm') and at the next righthand bend (**A**) strike straight ahead over a field (there is no footpath sign here) in a southerly direction towards the coppice. To the right in the foreground is a typical bit of English countryside — rolling fields dotted with trees, all very neat and ordered. In the distance is Woodbury Hill, an ancient British encampment occupied in 1405 by Owen Glendower who rose in revolt against Henry IV. Assisted by the French King he marched across Wales and onto Worcester which he plundered and burnt.

Cross the stile and follow the hedge on the left to the next stile. In the next field walk in a slightly south-westerly direction to the bridge and cross the bridge and stile. Keeping Keybridge Coppice on the left, proceed up the bank to Keybridge Farm. Go through the gate and make for the next stile, still keeping the wood on the left. Once over this stile turn left as you enter the field, still following the line of the wood. At the end of the cart track, walk diagonally to the gate at the righthand corner of Keybridge Plantation. Go through the gate and over the plank bridge, following the wood and hedgerow, and enter King's Wood through a gap, keeping to the left. At the end go through a gap in the hedge and double gates.

Carry on to the Droitwich — Kidderminster Road, keeping to the hedge on the righthand side. At this point a diversion to the right along the main road and then up a cul-de-sac to the left will bring you to Hampton Lovett Church, well worth seeing for its impressive Norman elements and the tombs guarding the remains of three interesting men. Sir John Pakington, a distinguished sixteenth-century lawyer, already owned Hampton Lovett Manor when he was given the nearby Westwood Park estate by Henry VIII. He built his great house next to Hampton Lovett Church but the manor was destroyed after the battle of Worcester and Westwood, then only a hunting lodge, became the family home.

Another Sir John, two centuries later, was quite a man: a high Tory, he terrified the Court, opposed the freedom of the press and the union of England and Scotland and denounced the bishops. He composed his own epitaph, describing himself as an indulgent father, a kind master and a charitable and loyal individual. Perhaps he was. Henry Hammond resides in the third tomb, royal chaplain to Charles 1, author of umpteen pamphlets and tracts and generally accepted as the father of biblical criticism.

At the main road turn left and along to the railway bridge. Under the bridge cross the road (with great care — a lot of the time it looks like the country road it still is but at times it is busy and most people drive too fast) and strike diagonally across the field to a bridge in the lefthand corner. Then head straight across the field to a stile to the left of a brick-and-tile house. Walk through the coppice and onto the road (Broad Alley, **B**).

Turn right and about 150 yards along the road turn left via a gate into a field. (If only all gates were like this). Fork slightly right to a stile in the righthand hedge just beyond the telegraph pole. Over the stile walk up this enormous field to a gate, keeping Addis Farmhouse to the right. Cross the road, climb the stile and walk straight ahead to a stile in the next hedge. Continue ahead in line with the telegraph poles to a stile. From this elevated point there are panoramic views — ahead the Lickeys, to the left the Clent Hills. Still walking in the same direction and keeping to the right of the poles, cross the stile and head down the slope. Cross the bridge over the brook and make for the stile on the road corner.

A short walk along this lane is Elmbridge Church, largely rebuilt in the nineteenth century but with a good Norman doorway and some twelfth-century pieces in the nave. It's a most attractive church in an attractive setting and the lovely little churchyard is well worth a stroll. The name of the church and parish has nothing to do with a bridge though. It comes from the Old English *elma, hrycg,* meaning a ridge of elm trees.

Turn right onto the road. 150 yards along the road enter a field on the corner and keep to the righthand hedgerow for some 200 yards as far as the gate and immediately turn 90° left (**C**) northwards across an open field towards the pylon and following the righthand hedge. Carry on to the kissing gate and then on to the next stile (Manor Farm ahead). Once over the stile keep to the lefthand hedge to a stile in the fence. Head north-west to a gated road, keeping the converted barns to the right.

At the road turn left and just past Mill House Farm (on the right) turn right over a stile into a field. Keeping to the fence on the right, cross the bridge and bear right across the field to the next bridge (behind the bushes) and over the brook turn right. In about 50 yards cross a rickety gate, pass a pumphouse (the brook is on the right), and on to a stile. Continue straight ahead through the field to the next stile. Over this, veer left, keeping the lake on the right, to a stile in the lefthand hedge towards the top of the field.

Head diagonally for the top lefthand corner of the field and cross the stile into Gateley Farm drive. Turn left and at the end of the drive right into Addis Lane. At the main road turn left and back to the start.

Walk 5
7 ½ miles

Neckless king and
Puritan divine

Inkberrow — Abbots Morton — Rous Lench — Inkberrow

OS Pathfinder Map   997 (SP 05/15)

Start and finish   Village green by the church (GR 015573) (If there is a wedding or service on try parking in Pepper Street or Stonepits Lane or up at the village hall.)

A beautiful walk through some really fine English countryside and taking in three interesting and attractive villages.

The walk starts in Inkberrow, a place which has changed a fair bit in recent years but which still retains a lot of its old character: brick and colour-washed houses, a small sloping green flanked by a black-and-white pub, and a church set among trees on a hill. From the village green, pass *The Old Bull* on the right (the model for *The Archers'* pub and well worth a visit) and then the crenellated old vicarage on the left (notice the enormous cedar tree) and the church of St Peter on the right.

The church was 'destructively restored' in 1840 and if you are into gargoyles there are some particularly grotesque ones over the porch. Inside the church there is an interesting display which sheds light on two intriguing episodes in its history. In May 1645 Charles I stayed at the old vicarage — on his way to defeat at Naseby — and left behind a book of military maps, which succeeding vicars have looked after. A century and a half later further evidence of that period was accidentally — not to say melodramatically — unearthed when, on a particularly filthy night, the local squire persuaded the Rev Heath to stay overnight. A sudden almighty thud at the head of his bed was found the next morning to have been caused by a large painting of Charles I which had fallen from its mounting behind the panelling. With the painting was a rather pathetic note purporting to be the confession of the King's anonymous executioner.

To the right of the display are two wooden screens, erected to create a vestry area. They are the work of Robert Pancheri of Bromsgrove and in his carving of Charles I you can see how ingeniously he has incorporated the king's execution. Not to be missed.

Carry on down the hill and at the bottom look back to see just how beautifully the church is set. Turn half right (where the road turns sharp left) and follow the footpath signposted Cladswell and Cookhill. Continue along the path to a stile and over this immediately turn right and climb a gate by a byre (a rather fine one with wooden managers) into the next field. At the other side of the field turn right through a wide opening and proceed in the same direction with the hedge on the lefthand side.

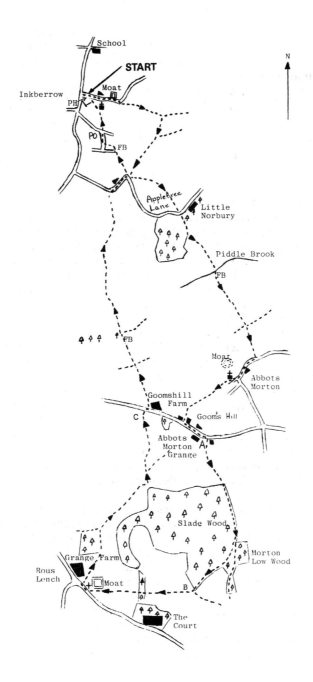

School

START

Moat

Inkberrow

PH

PO

FB

Appletree Lane

Little Norbury

Piddle Brook

FB

N

FB

Moat

Abbots Morton

Goomshill Farm

Gooms Hill

C

Abbots Morton Grange

A

Slade Wood

Grange Farm

Morton Low Wood

Rous Lench

Moat

B

The Court

27

Shortly, there is an opening on the left (by an oak tree). Go through this and carry on in the same direction, with the hedge now back on the righthand side. The path eventually becomes a bridleway and goes through a thicket until it passes two black-and-white cottage (the second in the winter of 1990/91 semi-derelict) and reaches the road. Turn left onto the road, immediately left again and go through a gate signposted Little Nobury and Knighton.

After a short steep climb the field divides. Take the lefthand side of the hedge (*ie* the hedge will be on your righthand side) and continue to a stile. The stile leads to a cultivated field which is not often walked — so the footpath across the field may not be very obvious. Look diagonally to the right for a stile in the hedge, which leads to the road, and make for this. Cross the road and go up the farm lane with a footpath sign.

About 200 yards along look for a footpath sign on the left, follow this and climb a stile into a field. Walk the length of the field, keeping the hedge on the left until near the bottom when you need to veer right to cross a rather dilapidated footbridge. Turn right over the bridge, go through an opening and turn left, keeping the hedge on the left until the second large gap. Go through this and proceed in the same direction between the hedge, now on the right, and a soft-wire fence on the left. Climb the wooden fence and continue past a paddock on the left and on to a stile near some modern timber-clad buildings and a small duck pond. Climb the stile, continue to the road and turn right towards the church.

Abbots Morton is one of England's oldest villages. It feels — and is — 'tucked away', hiding along the border with Warwickshire with two working farms in the middle. Originally called *Mortun* (or *Mortune*) the land was given to the Bishop of Worcester in 700 AD and then passed after the Conquest to the abbots of Evesham (hence its lengthened name). Nothing remains of the Saxon church that once stood here but much of today's building, with its distinctive squat tower and leaning porch, dates back to medieval times.

As you go through the churchyard notice to the right a former rector's tomb, perfectly protected by four great yew trees planted 130 years ago and now joined to form a green canopy. Leave the churchyard by a small gate at the end and cross the length of the field, keeping the hedge on the left until it ends and going through the gate facing. Turn left and proceed with the hedge on the left to a stile leading to a farmyard. Carry on and go through a gate onto the road.

Cross the road and turn left, passing Abbots Morton Manor and arriving at an unmarked footpath with a large barn at its entrance (**A**). Turn right onto this path and keep walking until you reach a gate into Slade Wood. The pathway through the wood is not always well defined and runs largely along its edge; so after going through the gate turn left and, as you walk uphill, keep as close to the perimeter as possible. You will emerge eventually at an old gate with signs of unfinished buildings just before it on the right.

Go through the gate into the next field, walking with the hedge on your left to just past the gate (about 100 yards); then turn 90° right (**B**) and head straight across the field to a narrow coppice. Go through the gateway (the gate itself was down at the end of 1990), then stop for a moment to take in a view which on a clear day can only be described as stunning: (from right to left) the Clent, Abberley amd Malvern Hills. Bear left over a grassy mound, past a little brick shelter on the left and downhill to another coppice. Climb a low wire fence in and out of the coppice.

Cross the large field/parkland. To the left is Rous Lench Court, best viewed by looking back just before entering the churchyard. Some of the house goes back to Tudor times though much is modern (a lot of the original building having been pulled down nearly 200 years ago). Some years ago Rolt described the Court's clipped yew hedges as probably the best example of 'extensive, ancient and elaborate topiary work' in England. The house's most distinguished visitor was Richard Baxter, the seventeenth-century Puritan divine from Kidderminster who during his stay wrote the first part of the most famous of his works — *The Saints' Everlasting Rest* — and dedicated the book to Sir Thomas and Lady Rous.

Enter the churchyard through a small metal gate and walk past the church. Better still, go inside. It is bigger than it seems and though partly restored in the last century has some fine Norman work still — the arches on the south side, the south doorway; and a surprising splash of 'medieval' brilliance which was in fact carried out by Florentine craftsmen in 1885.

From the churchyard take the exit to the road, turn right into the village street and just before the pretty village green turn right again at the public footpath sign which takes you through the garden of a private house. Rous is the largest of the Lenches (*lench* from the Old English meaning 'hill'), nestling among these lovely wooded hills and so far untouched by motorways and the general roar of life.

Climb the stile into a large field and, bearing slightly right, head for a gate (the lefthand of two gates); and, over this, make for another gate/opening in the righthand corner of the field. Pass through this and two more gates, keeping the hedge to the right. Bear left up a well defined bridleway, and with the hedge and ditch on the left, carry on, passing through another (broken down) metal gate and arriving at the road (**C**).

Turn right, cross the road and in a few yards turn left through a gate with the farmhouse (Goomshill) and hedge on the right. At the end of this field is a cultivated field. Cross the field in a straight line to a footbridge over a stream and continue in the same direction up a steep bank through a wooded area. Climb the stile, follow the field round to the right and at the top righthand corner amongst some trees there is a stile (next to a sawn-down telegraph pole, now a mere 5' high).

Ahead is a very large cultivated field. Head for a clump of trees, keeping in the same general direction, towards the lefthand corner of the field. Just beyond this is another field; keep the hedge on your left at first and then leave the hedge and head for the corner of the field and an easily seen stile. Over the stile, keep the hedge on the right, following it right to the end. Turn left, still with the hedge on the right, climb a stile attached to a tree and turn sharp right. Keep the ditch on the right and make for a stile in the corner which leads onto a lane.

Turn right and stay on the lane until you reach a gate signposted Pepper Street. Through the gate, keep the brook on the left until a crossing point is reached, then cross and carry on in the same general direction, but bearing slightly left, to a stile in the hedge. The stile leads into a narrow path between two rows of houses and, at the end, a road. Turn right at the road, and follow it round as it bears left. Turn down the road on the right opposite the post office and down some steps which lead eventually to the church.

Walk through the churchyard and turn left back to the green.

Walk 6   *A circle round Belbroughton*

11 miles (*or* **two separate walks of 4 miles and 7 miles)**
Hollies Hill — Walton Hill — Drayton — Hollies Hill
OS Pathfinder Map (SO 87/97)
Start and finish   Layby on the A491 (north side) between the
                       Belbroughton turning and the *Holy Bush Inn*
                       (GR 929781)

A walk that begins by heading for the hills — but is really not that strenuous — then circles around Belbroughton. Walton Hill rises to 1000 feet, part of the Clent Hills which range from Kinver Edge to the Lickeys. Most of the Clent area is owned by the National Trust or is green belt or conservation land; so with a bit of luck its natural beauty will be allowed to flourish. If you plan to walk the bridleways of Clent in the winter be warned - they can be fairly muddy.

The walk starts at a stile just past the Stourbridge end of the layby. Head towards Walton Hill across the field and then alongside a hedge on the left. Join the farm track, bear left and follow it to a lane. Cross the lane to a stile just to the right and continue the climb until you join the bridleway which bears right up to Walton Hill. On reaching the open area keep ahead to the *trig point* (1035 feet/315 metres) where on a clear day there are tremendous views over the surrounding countryside. Walton Hill dominates the eastern section of the Clent Hills Country Park just as Adam's Hill, slightly lower, dominates in the west; and the area's visitors go back a long way: the Ancient Britons left some of their flint arrowheads here and several Bronze Age burial mounds were excavated in the eighteenth century — and unfortunately destroyed. In the middle ages the hills would have been crossed by pilgrims on thier way to St Kenelm's shrine; and nowadays they are extremely popular with Midland walkers.

The *trig point* is the most northerly spot on the walk; so head back south now and follow the waymarked North Worcestershire Path (*see* Walk 14 for a note about this path) along the track towards Waltonhill Farm. A stile next to the farm entrance leads to the distinct waymarked track (with benches for a rest) and a new plantation on the slopes on the left. Proceed until Calcothill Farm can be seen. At the next stile leave the North Worcestershire Path and go ahead to the stile on the right. Continue past the farm buildings on the left and over a stile where a plaque on a large boulder indicates it has come from Wales, deposited here by a glacier.

Turn left onto the bridleway and follow the concrete drive down as far as the house, turning right onto another bridleway. Carry on to a

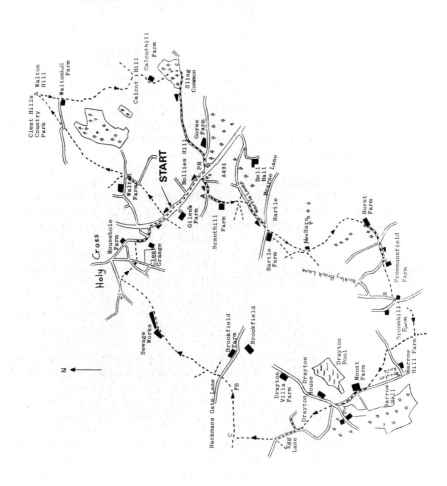

32

lane and turn right to the *Holly Bush Inn* where you can either decide you've had enough for one day and carry on back to the layby *or* take a welcome break and continue with the rest of the walk which is quite different in character.

Take care when crossing the main road, then go right to the lane which runs down the side of *The Four Winds* (Dark Lane). After a short distance turn left into a farm drive which is also a bridleway (**A**), pass Branthill Farm and then walk between two pools and across the field to Hartle Lane. Turn right into the lane and after a few yards left onto a bridleway just before Hartle Farm.

If you have the time this is the point on the walk from which two interesting little excursions can be made. In Domesday there were two distinct settlements here: *Beolne* (from an old river name, perhaps after the plant henbane) and *Broctun* ('the town on the brook'). Turn left, instead of right, along Hartle Lane for the site of the deserted village of Belne where there are earthworks and the remains of a Norman chapel. Turn right along Hartle Lane and on into today's Belbroughton, a large and very pleasant village with more than its fair share of attractive old buildings. For over four hundred years it was known for its manufacture of scythes, its reputation becoming worldwide by the nineteenth century. The church is also very distinctive: it has two naves and chancels.

Back on the main walk pass Hartle Farm and carry on as far as New Barn (partly demolished). Leave the bridleway here and keep close round the righthand side of the wall to the stile on the right. Follow the hedgerow, keeping it on the left. Climb the next stile and, with the hedgerow now on your right, climb another stile. Follow the line of trees and continue along a hedgerow, following the path heading towards Hurst Farm which you pass on the left.

Turn right onto a track leading to Hockley Brook Lane. Follow the lane round to the right, bearing immediately left just past Freemansfield Farm. Take the stile in the left in the holly hedge and, keeping the farm buildings on the left, proceed to a gate in the hedge and then down the slope to a stile. Over the stile, walk up the slope to the white house on the brow of the hill (**B**).

On reaching Dordale Road turn left and at the next road junction take the footpath opposite between two bungalows. Over the stile at the far end turn right and follow the hedge for about 100 yards to a stile on the right. Descend a slope and if you are lucky you may see a heron fishing in the pool on your left. Go over a stile in the righthand corner of the field and in about 25 yards turn right at a gap in the hedge with a piece of iron railing acting as a stile; then negotiate the 'stile' in the lefthand corner of the small field. (It is to be hoped these two obstacles will soon be replaced by more conventional stiles.) In the field turn right and follow a line of trees to the lane.

Cross the lane to the stile on the bank opposite and bear half left over the brow of the hill and down through a gate halfway between trees in the hedge opposite a stile at the bottom lefthand corner of the field, emerging into the lane just past the power lines. Turn right past Mount Farm and follow the lane to Drayton (where a slight detour to the left brings you to the *Robin Hood* and refreshments).

120 years ago some members of the Worcestershire Naturalists' Club were also walking in the area, enjoying a heated discussion about the origin of the *Berrow* (a tumulus on Barrow Hill just to the south of this walk). But they didn't have to look for refreshments:

> The hospitable occupant of Drayton Court,
> Mr Pearman, stopped the naturalists as they
> passed, to show them a specimen of rock,
> and then kindly improvised a lunch, which
> was by no means unacceptable.

The party walked on through Belbroughton, across the Clent Hills and down into Hagley where they enjoyed a late-afternoon dinner at the *Lyttleton Arms*. What a life.

Back in the lane carry on past the junction with Drayton Road to a footpath on the left up a bank just past the houses. At the top of the slope head towards the nearest large tree and then follow the line of trees to Egg Lane. Turn right and after about 300 yards, where the lane bends left, go through the gate and follow the hedge, first on the left and then on the right. At the T-junction of paths (**C**) turn right, ignoring the stile and footpath sign on the left. Follow the hedge on the left to where it ends, then go straight ahead and aim for the house on the ridge ahead.

You will soon see the next stile. Climb this and continue in the same line to another stile. Cross a footbridge and stile and head towards some trees on the skyline and a stile that leads into Hackmans Gate Lane. Cross the lane and follow the bridleway opposite all the way to the Holy Cross Children's Play Area on the right. Turn right alongside the wooden fence and through the allotments to the road. Cross this and Holy Cross Lane ahead to a footpath opposite (alongside a bungalow). At the end turn right onto the main road (Bromsgrove Road). Turn right where the road joins the bypass and back — taking great care — to the start.

Walk 7   *A view from the bridge*
10 miles *or* **6½ miles**
Lydiate Ash — Upton Warren
OS Pathfinder Maps   953 (SO 86/96) & 974 (SO 87/97)
Start   The junction of Woodrow Lane and the A38 at
                               Lydiate Ash (GR 970749 on map 953). Park on the
                               wide grass verge at the end of Woodrow Lane.
Finish   The *Swan Inn* at Upton Warren (GR 933675 on
                               map 974)

A ramble over motorway footbridges — surely a contradiction in terms? In fact, this linear walk, crossing all the footbridges over the M5 and M42 along the route, happily illustrates how most of the old footpath network has survived the onslaught of the motorway. It's a very interesting walk and from the footbridges offers some excellent wide views over the countryside.

Before setting out check the times of Midland Red buses that travel between Worcester and Birmingham (if you can't get someone to drive you back). Please note, too, that older maps do not show some of the detail on this route: even the current 953 doesn't show the M5/M42 junction.

From the A38 follow Woodrow Lane to a drive on the righthand side of Woodrow Nurseries, also signposted to a Caravan Club site. Take the drive past the nurseries, then walk straight on across a field to a stile in the motorway fence. Turn right and follow a fenced path over the first footbridge of the walk, then bear left to the motorway fence and a stile. Carry straight on to a blue farm gate and then along the obvious footpath across two more stiles, and, with the Blue Cross Animal Sanctuary on the right, to Wildmoor Lane. Turn left along the lane to a stile on the right immediately before a motorway bridge.

Follow a fenced path to a stile at the end, then bear right to cross the three fences. The first of these doesn't have a stile at present but can be negotiated by turning back parallel to the motorway as far as a gate, then turning left and back to the correct line. Cross the next two fences normally — *ie* at the stiles — and proceed to a footbridge over a small stream (Battlefield Brook flows from Chadwick and joins Spadesbourne Brook in Bromsgrove to form the River Salwarpe) which will be recrossed later.

Cross a field heading towards Meadow Farm and, keeping the white-painted building on the right, pass through a wooden gate into a farm drive. Turn left and follow the drive to the B4091 (Stourbridge Road); then turn left and recross the motorway. Pass the *Plough and Harrow*

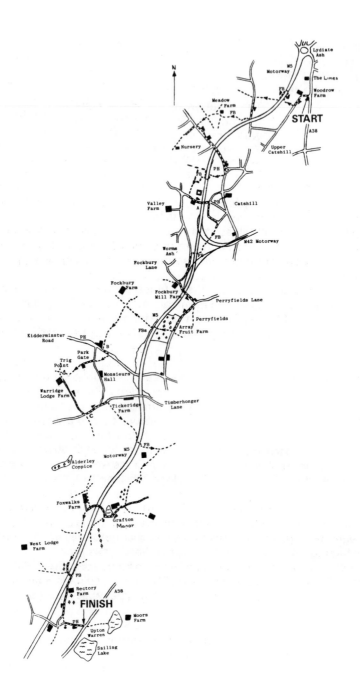

N

Lydiate
Ash

M5
Motorway

The Limes

Woodrow
Farm

FB

START

A38

Meadow
Farm

FB

Upper
Catshill

Nursery

FB

PH

Valley
Farm

PH

Catshill

A

Worms
Ash

FB

M42 Motorway

Fockbury
Lane

Fockbury
Farm

Fockbury
Mill Farm

Perryfields Lane

M5

Perryfields

FBs

Array
Fruit Farm

Kidderminster
Road

PH

Park
Gate

B

Trig
Point

A

Monsieurs
Hall

Warridge
Lodge Farm

Tickeridge
Farm

Timberhonger
Lane

C

FB

M5
Motorway

Alderley
Coppice

Foxwalks
Farm

Grafton
Manor

West Lodge
Farm

FB

Rectory
Farm

A38

FINISH

Moors
Farm

PH

Upton
Warren

Sailing
Lake

36

on the right and on the left Christ Church where A E Housman was baptised, his grandfather was the first vicar and his parents and grandparents are buried.

Follow the main road for a further 200 yards, then turn right to a footpath opposite house no. 284. This steeply rising path passes the cemetery to a stile at the top. Over this, cross the field to another stile by the motorway fence, turn left over the stile and then cross the second motorway footbridge. At this point the OS map shows the footpath going right alongside the motorway and then left before crossing the field ahead. But it is easier to go ahead at the stile and then follow the 'permissive' path along the hedge on the left, turning left and then right to a gap just past a holly bush in the hedge. Turn left and with the hedge on the right proceed to Rocky Lane (**A**).

Many who live in this part of Worcestershire may feel — justifiably — that they've got more than their fair share of motorway building. For the rambler there are more positive features: the evidence of recent years, for example, that the motorway's largely undisturbed banks and verges attract and support wildlife; and the view from the footbridges, some of them unique, over the changing countryside.

Head left back across the motorway and then right down Hinton Fields at Penny Pot Cottage. Follow this lane taking a sharp lefthand bend to a T-junction and then follow a signposted bridleway on the right to the motorway junction. Cross the first carriageway of the M42 and then go under the second and up to a gate. Take the lefthand gate and follow the bridleway by the fence on the right down to cross the footbridge over the M5 and join Bumblehole Lane. Turn left and follow the track to Fockbury Lane, bearing left back over the motorway to Perryfields Lane. Do not cross Perryfields Lane at this stage but follow the Housman Trail sign (This is the way Housman walked to school in Bromsgrove when he lived at Fockbury House) using the grass verge on the right until it ends just before Array Fruit Farm.

Cross to the verge on the left and carry on until you see a large metal gate on the right. Cross back to the kissing gate and a drive and then follow the green track to the fifth motorway footbridge. Cross and descend the steps to a stile and then bear right down to a footpath over Battlefield Brook.

Follow the clearly marked footpath ahead across two fields to a fence and stile on the brow of the hill. Do not cross the stile but turn left and, keeping the fence on the right, continue to a stile. Cross the stile and follow the hedge on the left for 50 yards to the point where it turns sharp left; then bear right down the slope across the field to a ditch crossing between two stiles. Bear left across the next field, crossing a bridge to a fence/stile on the left. Cross the fence and then with the hedge on the right head up the slope over another stile and bear slightly left, passing Battlefield Farm on the right, to the signposted stile onto the A448 Kidderminster Road (**B**). Turn left towards Bromsgrove.

For the shorter walk simply carry on into Bromsgrove (about 1¼ miles) and to the Midland Red bus that will take you back to the start.

For the main walk go along the A448 for about 200 yards as far as a signpost and stile on the right. Cross the stile and the field to another stile by a holly tree; then carry on to a stile in Monsieurs Hall Lane. Cross the lane to the drive of Warridge House and passing to the right of the house go through a wooden gate to a track towards Warridge Lodge Farm. After passing the next gate bear right away from the track for a short distance to a *trig point* from where in clear weather there are surprisingly good views of the Malvern, Abberley and Woodbury Hills and the Welsh hills beyond. Carry on past the pillar for a few yards and then turn sharply left to the side of Warridge Lodge Farm. Pass to the left of the farm and then go through a gate and along the farm driveway to the junction with Timberhonger Lane (**C**).

Turn left and carry on, passing the end of Monsieurs Hall Lane on the left. *Take care* along the next 100 yards of narrow lane to a stile seen at the top of some steps on the bank to the right. Over this stile, head straight on for a few yards to the brow of the hill when the next stile can be seen in the fence ahead to the right of a wood. Keep straight on and, passing a small copse and three oak trees on the left, reach a farm track alongside the motorway. Turn right and then cross the motorway into East Lodge Farm driveway.

Immediately on leaving the bridge look for a stile on the left. Cross it and another stile with the hedge on the left; and then bear right to the top of the field and the farm drive. Turn left along the driveway to where it crosses a cattle-grid at the hedge, turn right down the slope and then follow the hedge on the left for ¼ mile to a gate on the left below the farm. Through the gate, go right and left to a stile on the right just before the trees. Follow the line of the stream and trees on the left to a stile into a plantation of fir trees. Then, keeping the wooden fence on the left, head towards the wood-faced building, cross a stile and then a second stile by a gate into a drive, and go through a woden gate past Grafton Cottage to the lane (Grafton Lane).

Bromsgrove was once described as lying 'not far from Grafton'. That's how important the latter once was. The manor of Grafton has always been in powerful hands, owned by William the Conqueror's cousin, the influential Staffords and then for 450 years the Talbot family. During the long years when adherence to any religious body other than the Anglican Church was both dangerous and decidedly disadvantageous Grafton Manor remained the centre for Catholicism in

East Worcestershire. (**See** Walk 9). The manor house was rebuilt in the 1560s but a fire in 1710 destroyed a lot of that fine Elizabethan building. In recent years the present owners — hoteliers — have undertaken a great deal of restoration work and some of the sixteenth-century building has been preserved.

Turn right and follow the lane past the manor house and the fishponds (with the ruins of the old icehouse) and over the motorway towards Foxwalks Farm. (As someone recently remarked: 'It must be nice to feel you've got you own motorway bridge'.) Where the driveway turns right towards the farm, go left through a gateway and follow a gravel track across the field to a fence. Do not cross the fence but turn left and go straight on through a metal gate; and cross the field roughly parallel to the motorway, heading towards the towers of the BBC's Droitwich transmitter in the distance. At the fence go through the metal gate and follow the green lane to cross the motorway for the last time on the Rectory Farm bridge.

Follow the track past the farm to the lane and continue until you see Upton Warren church in the distance and a stile on the left. Cross the stile and then head across the field towards the church, leaving the field via a kissing gate into the lane. Turn left and follow the lane back to the A38, the *Swan Inn* and the bus back to the start.

Walk 8
Either side of the Saltway

14 miles *or* **11½ miles** *or* **6 miles**
Walkwood — Bradley Green — Feckenham — Walkwood
OS Pathfinder Map   974 (SO 86/96) & 975 (SP 06/16)
Start and finish   Morton Stanley Park (GR 031653 on SP 06/16)

This walk is the ultimate in flexibility, offering two shorter alternatives for those with less energy or time. It would be a particular pity however to miss either Feckenham or the Bradley Green area and walkers can work out for themselves even further alternatives involving the southern part of the route.

Morton Stanley Park on the very western edge of Redditch is a popular venue for children and dogwalkers — so look out for both! The really energetic might be tempted to do a circuit of the 'Trim Trail' as a pre-walk warm-up.

Walk the length of the paved path (about ¾ mile) at the end of which are sports' changing rooms and public toilets. Turn left along Green Lane and right at the crossroads towards Elcock's Brook. Pass Sillins Hall on the left and walk straight up the short hill passing the *Brook Inn* on the left. Near the brow of the hill turn left into a field at a footpath sign; and, keeping the hedge on the right, climb the stile on the right at the top of the field, skirt round a poultry house and go through a gate into a drive. Turn left when you reach the road (Cruisehill Lane) and walk towards point **A** on the map.

For the short walk (6 miles) turn down the bridleway on the left (**A**) to some houses (a little area shown as Tricks's Hole on older maps) and join the main walk at point **E** for the return via Norgrove Court.

For the main walk continue on the road to the top of Cruise Hill (there's a little chapel on the left) and bear right into Burial Lane at the bridleway signposted to Morton Underhill and Feckenham. Stay on the bridleway descending the hill until eventually you pass through a small metal gate and reach a bridleway junction (**B**).

This is the best place to make a diversion to the fascinating village of Feckenham, an excellent example of a village that has managed to escape the 'development' which has hit so many other parts of the county. It's a gem of a place, almost every building of some interest. It was for several centuries the seat of forest jurisdiction, giving its name to the Royal Forest which stretched as far as Worcester and overlapped into Warwickshire. It grew up around the king's lodge and court house (which also housed the prison) and was a busy medieval market centre when Redditch was an obscure village. Geoffrey Chaucer, one of the Forest Keepers, once resided near the church.

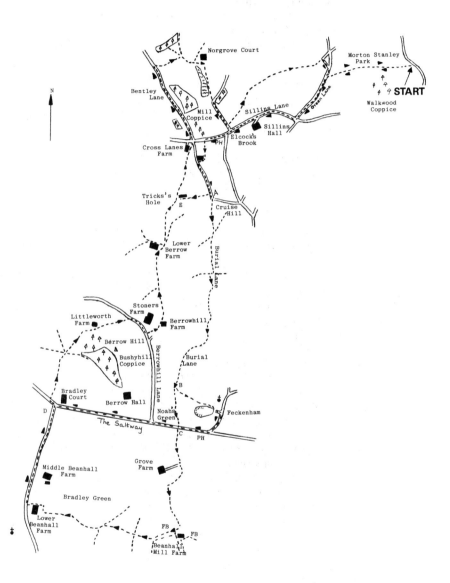

Norgrove Court

Morton Stanley
Park

START

Walkwood
Coppice

Bentley
Lane

Mill
Coppice

Sillins Lane

Sillins
Hall

Elcock's
Brook

Green Lane

Cross Lanes
Farm

PH

Tricks's
Hole

E

A

Cruise
Hill

Lower
Berrow
Farm

Burial Lane

Stoners
Farm

Littleworth
Farm

Berrowhill
Farm

Berrow Hill

Bushyhill
Coppice

Berrowhill Lane

Burial
Lane

Bradley
Court

Berrow Hall

B

Noahs
Green

Feckenham

D

The Saltway

C

PH

Middle Beanhall
Farm

Grove
Farm

Bradley Green

Lower
Beanhall
Farm

FB

FB

Beanhall
Mill Farm

N

The church has been much restored and repaired over the centuries but still has its medieval tower and windows and a 700-year-old arcade; and to the south-west of the church is a ditch which surrounded the prison for offenders against the harsh forest laws. But there is a variety of other building styles in the village — half-timbered, whitewashed, red brick — and there are remains of its industrial past, such as the arresting building opposite the green, once a needle factory.

If you decide to visit Feckenham — for its attractions *and* its refreshments — rejoin the main walk simply by walking up the main road to point **C** on the map. Otherwise continue straight on from point **B** on a pleasant bridleway alongside Bow Brook to reach the B4090 at Brook House, Noah's Green. The latter has nothing to do with any great floods of the past but comes from the Old English *atten, ofer* meaning 'at' or 'by a hill'.

For the medium walk (11½ miles) turn right onto the road at Noah's Green and walk towards Hanbury. This road has been known for centuries as the Saltway. There were probably a dozen or more salt roads running out of Droitwich, the only area in Central England producing salt in the Middle Ages. But this and the one running north to Birmingham and south to Worcester and Gloucester were the best known; and carters with their loaded packhorses would have been a familiar sight along here, many of them trying to work out ways around Feckenham so that they could avoid paying tolls to the lord of the manor.

Rejoin the main route by turning right onto the bridleway to Tinker's Hall and Perry Mill (**D**).

For the main walk cross the road and follow a paved bridleway signposted Morton Underhill, passing a broken windpump on the right. Enter a field gate ahead by Grove Farm entrance on the right. The path bears right, then left, then right again towards the brook. Keep the brook on the left, pass the first footbridge (bridleway to Morton Underhill) and at the second footbridge leave the brook (*ie don't* cross over), *ignore* a small gate and instead follow the field hedge curving to the right.

Keep the hedge on the left as far as a small wooden gate, turn immediately left over a footbridge and continue with the fence, hedge and stream on the right. (On the left there is a view of the tower of Bradley Green Church.) Approach the rear of Lower Beanhall Farm, turn right through a gate into a field and then left up to a small wooden gate in the centre of fencing. Pass straight through an orchard and on to the road, turning right to walk through the hamlet.

Bradley Green is an interesting little place, with a surprising number of buildings. Its nineteenth-century church (back up to the left) stands on the site of a much more ancient chapel for Bradley was a manor 1200 years ago, originally owned by the King of Mercia. On the right you pass Middle Beanhill Farm, a fine example of sixteenth-century half-timbered building. The 'hall' element in Upper, Middle and Lower Beanhall, incidentally, may mislead. It's from the Old English *healh* meaning 'nook of land'. Clearly this was the place to grow lots of good beans.

Carry on to the junction with the B4090 (the Saltway again), passing the post office on the left. Turn left towards Hanbury and cross the road to the bridleway signposted Tinker's Hall and Perry Mill (**D**). At a junction of bridleways climb a fence on the left and cross to a stile/fence on the right. Proceed diagonally across a field towards a striped black-and-white marker (there's a pool on the left). Cross the stile and head for a metal gate in the top left by a water trough. Emerge onto the grass verge alongside a gravel drive to a road (Berrowhill Lane). Turn right and walk about ¼ mile to a footpath sign, then left up the drive of Berrowhill Farm.

Bear left into a field, skirting a new bungalow on the right and continuing with a hedge on the right. Drop down on the right of an old hedge line and pass through a gap in the hedge. Cross left of a power pole in the centre and walk under pylon cables to the corner of a field hedge on the left. Go through a metal gate and cross the next field to a gap into a green lane, bearing right to a gate. Cross a concrete drive, aiming up the hill between two trees; then descend to a gate and cross to another gate. Head up the field to a gate onto a bridleway by some houses (**E**).

Pass to the left of Broadgate Cottage and go through a gate to a green track. Walk down the drive of Cross Lanes Farm to emerge at a crossroads. Cross over the road and walk up the hill, signposted to Bentley. Pass Park Cottage on the left and by some metal railings go through a gate on the right down an unpaved drive to Norgrove Court, one of the first houses in the county to be built of brick. It lies low and moated and surrounded by former fish ponds. It is said to have hidden Charles II after the battle of Worcester and had a reputation in the past for being haunted by pre-1649 ghosts!

Stay on the drive, with a view of the house on the left. Go through a wooden wicket gate onto the main paved drive, emerging over a cattle-grid; and bear right onto the road, continuing until just before a road junction. Take the path on the left through a metal gate, following a line of trees, then a brook, on the right. Cross the stiles, keeping the brook on the right, then climb a stile into a paddock. Climb another stile into a drive (with a footpath sign in the hedge); then turn right onto a road (Green Lane) and at the Morton Stanley changing rooms and toilets turn left and back to the car park — either along the paved path or through the woods via the nature trail.

Walk 9   *The Catholic Connection*

6 miles
Purshull Green — Randan Wood — Chaddesley Wood — Purshull Green
OS Pathfinder Map   953 (SO 87/97)
Start and finish   The grass verge on the north side of the A448
                          Kidderminster — Bromsgrove road (GR 903726)

A gentle walk through the quiet countryside lying either side of the A448, farming land in the southern part of the route, woods that were once part of Feckenham Forest in the second half of the walk, the whole area still largely untouched by modern development (pylons apart).

Begin by walking along the road towards Bromsgrove for about 200 yards and opposite Outwood Farm cross over *with great care* to the signposted stile just past the farmhouse. Climb the stile and follow the hedge on the right through a gate and at the next gate go straight across the field to the stile-and-ditch crossing just past the pylon. Over the stile follow the hedge on the right leading into an orchard, turn left and, passing to the right of the cottage, emerge onto the open land of Purshull Green (near another pylon).

Pushull is an intriguing name and nobody seems quite prepared to be categorical about its origin. The best suggestion is that it means 'Pyrti's hill' though who Pyrti was we will never know and the hill is a very little one. Quiet though it may be today, this whole area has witnessed dangerous times, caught up in the mainstream of religious and political strife; for due south of here is Purshull Hall, which was once part of the network of Roman Catholic houses in East Worcestershire. A little to the north-west of here is Harvington Hall where Father John Wall had his headquarters; nearer still, to the south-west, is Rushock Court where he was captured (**see** Walk 1). Due east of the Hall is Badge Court, confiscated from the Wyntour family after the Gunpowder Plot, but a Catholic stronghold for centuries; and beyond that the most important of all, Grafton Manor, the controlling centre.

Bear left, cross the drive and follow the path between the houses towards the pond. After 150 yards look carefully for a stile by a gate in the hedge on the left just before the next buildings. (Bear right across the open space to view the pond and birds.) Climb the stile into the next field and follow the hedge on the right to the old bridge in the corner.

In the next field go straight up the slope (again, the hedge shown to the right on the OS map has disappeared), passing the old pond on the right. Descend the hill and go slightly right under the power cables to cross a fence by the hedge on the left. Follow this hedge on the left uphill

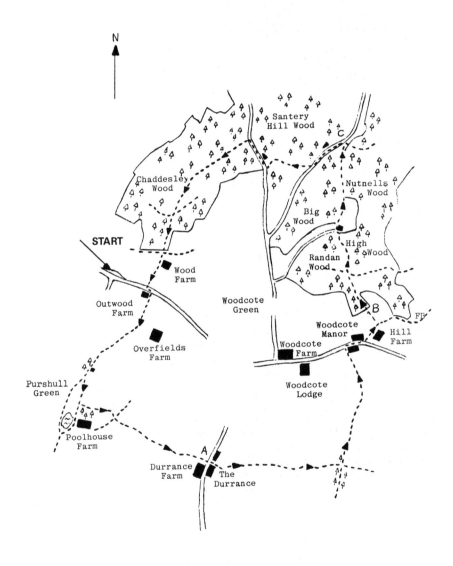

N

Santery
Hill Wood

C

Chaddesley
Wood

Nutnells
Wood

Big
Wood

High
Wood

Randan
Wood

START

Wood
Farm

Outwood
Farm

Woodcote
Green

B

FP

Overfields
Farm

Woodcote
Manor

Hill
Farm

Woodcote
Farm

Purshull
Green

Woodcote
Lodge

Poolhouse
Farm

A

Durrance
Farm

The
Durrance

45

to another stile in the corner. In the next field go straight ahead to a track leading down to a farm bridge and over this bear left to a stile on the bank to the left of the orchard. Then follow the hedge on the right up to the gate into the road at Durrance Farm (**A**).

Cross over to the yard opposite and go through two gates to the track which swings to the left under pylons and on to a gate. Through the gate keep the hedge on the left and carry on through two fields to an unusual metal stile leading down to a sunken track. Turn left through a gate and follow the bridleway with the hedge first on the left and then on the right, past the farm to the A448. Turn right and again with great care (this road attracts a higher than average number of dangerous drivers) cross over to Woodcote Manor House.

The manor's origin goes back beyond the Conquest but in the seventeenth century it was owned by Stephen Lyttleton, one of the Gunpowder Plot conspirators — so here we catch up with the Catholic connection again. It's not surprising that the whole sorry episode occupies such an important place in Worcestershire history for a high proportion of the county's leading families at that time were Roman Catholic. The leading plotter, Robert Catesby, was a cousin of the Wyntour brothers of Huddington Court (south-east of Droitwich) and he and Stephen managed to evade capture for some time before being caught at Hagley Hall and, like the others, hung in 1606 for their involvement. (Read John Humphrey's *Studies in Worcestershire History* for a very good account of the conspiracy.)

Pass Woodcote Manor House and turn left into a wide field entrance. Here a narrow track between two hedges (with the house drive on the right) leads into a field. The hill on the left (**B**) gives a good view of the Worcestershire hills — Bredon, the Malverns and the Abberley Hills — and of the Welsh hills beyond. Walk up into Randan Wood and High Wood, following the track down the slope and then up past the beech trees to a path crossing. Carry straight over here, walking slightly uphill and emerging from the woods by Highwood Cottage.

Pass in front of the cottage and enter a fenced bridleway which follows the edge of the field and then enters Nutnells Wood at a gate. Follow the rather muddy track to the road (**C**).

At the road turn left for ¼ mile and then bear right up a drive where, by the side of a garage, a stile leads into Santery Hill Wood. Follow the sunken path to the road, turn right and then after ¼ mile turn left onto the 'permissive' Jubilee Drive through Chaddesley Wood. Follow the drive through the woods past the buildings and several cross-paths to the junction of paths near a post for information booklets. At this point take the track ahead and slightly left down the hill to the lane which leads past a small pond and to the main road. Turn right back to the parking place.

Walk 10

A mere stroll

8 *or* 6 miles
Mere Green — Puck Hill — Dean Brook — Mere Green
OS Pathfinder Map 974 (SO 86/96)

Start and finish   Roadside verge at Mere Green on the B4090
                         (GR 953624)

A stroll through the parishes of Hanbury and Hadzor, the hilly and wooded area to the east of Droitwich. Modern Hanbury, 12 square miles in size, centres around the *Vernon Arms* at the dangerous bend on the B4090; but its wonderfully sited church is visible to most of its scattered population and the parish has more than its fair share of interesting historic houses, two of which can be seen on this walk.

It is probably fair to say the parish of Hadzor is generally less well known. Though similar in character it is a fraction of Hanbury's size, has nothing to compare with the likes of Hanbury or Mere Hall. But there is something of interest in every square mile of this county and through this secluded little parish run the old Saltway, the railway, orginally the Birmingham and Gloucester, and the Worcester — Birmingham Canal; and though not so visible it has a fine little church, mainly fourteenth-century, with a medieval sundial.

To reach the start drive along the Droitwich — Alcester road and stop on the verge, directly down from Mere Hall and 100 yards past the signpost to Broughton Green and Earl's Common.

Climb the stile by the footpath sign (there's a pond to the right) and make a mental note of the footbridge directly opposite as this will be the return route. Aim across the field in a direction left of diagonal, keeping left of a small fenced area. Don't take the obvious path going to an opening but instead make for a wooden stile and enter a newly planted wood. Head directly across to a footbridge and continue, with a hedge on the right, to another stile.

Turn immediately right, climb a stile and follow the hedge on the right. Go over another stile and before reaching the end of the next large field look for a red metal gate on the right. Go through and cross a narrow field to another metal gate. The path then takes a quarter circle right to a stile. Over this stile, turn left and follow the hedge on the left to a small metal gate and then on to the next metal gate. Keeping the same direction pass the edge of Broughton Wood; and at the end go through a gate on the left and turn right to follow the hedge on the right through two metal gates. Continue bearing slightly left (and under some barbed wire) and through a metal gate to the road at Broughton Green (**A**).

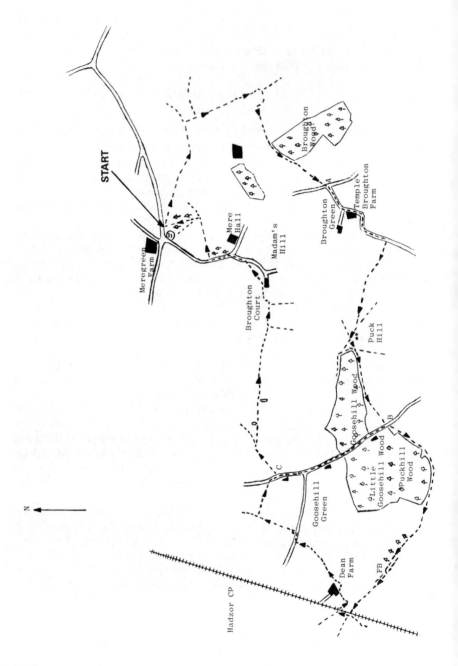

N

START

Meregreen Farm

Mere Hall

Broughton Court

Madam's Hill

Broughton Wood

Broughton Green

Temple Broughton Farm

Puck Hill

Goosehill Wood

Little Goosehill Wood

Puckhill Wood

Goosehill Green

Dean Farm

FB

Hadzor CP

C

B

48

Follow the road opposite, signposted Earl's Common, Himbleton and Crowle; and after ½ mile look for a field entry going off to the right just before the road starts to descend steeply (the second dip, not the first). There is a footpath sign by a stile just up the track and at this point the route joins the Wychavon Way, a 40-mile path stretching from Holt Fleet to Winchcombe in the Cotswolds. It *should* be clearly marked with yellow arrows and crowns but most of these are currently missing.

Climb the stile and follow the path along the top of Puck Hill with the hedge on the right. It's a lovely name though of uncertain origin. It may mean 'goblin' or 'watersprite' from the Old English *puca*. Approaching a cottage, veer right over a double stile to pass the cottage (now on the left). Then, after a caravan on the left, turn left over another double stile and right to follow the hilltop again with the hedge on the right. Go over a stile and take a diagonal path across a field (at the end of 1990 ploughed) to a stile just visible in the hedge and so reach a lane (**B**).

For the shorter walk turn right and follow the lane for ½ mile. Past the turning to Shernal Green (on the left) look for a metal gate just beyond a bungalow (**C**).

For the longer walk from (**B**) go through a metal gate directly opposite the stile and follow the path along the edge of Puckhill Wood. In the second field, about halfway along, look for a Wychavon Way marker post in the edge of the wood. The yellow arrow points diagonally left to a large oak tree, with a yellow mark, in the left corner of the field. Climb the stile to the left of the tree into a narrow strip of woodland which runs alongside Dean Brook.

It is very overgrown here and it may be necessary to get into the field on the right and proceed along the edge with the strip of wood on the left. Enter the wood where it broadens and follow a meandering path by the brook. Turn left at the stile with a yellow arrow and cross a footbridge. (The route now leaves the Wychavon Way but encounters it again for a short distance beyond the railway line.) Turn right and follow the brook for ½ mile to a stile in the corner of a field.

Cross the stile, climb the steps and go over the railway line (noting the 'Caution' sign). Down the other side, turn right over a footbridge and follow the railway embankment. Turn right and go through a tunnel under the railway. Looking at the line of the railway on a map is intriguing to say the least. It runs a mile east of Bromsgrove centre, a mile-and-a-half east of Droitwich and more than two miles east of the centre of Worcester, the result of the promotors' total indifference to any needs the county might have had. For in 1840 the directors of the Birmingham and Gloucester Railway Company were interested only in the quickest way to get the Midlands' goods to the port of Bristol and on to the growing

Empire. For years horse buses filled the gap between towns and stations until further railway building solved the problem — at least for Worcester and Droitwich. Complaints at Bromsgrove can still be heard.

Go under a wire and veer right to follow the remains of a hedge. Pass through a large metal gate and turn left (ignoring a small gate by the brook). Keep the hedge on the left but veer slightly right to pass Dean Farm. With the hedge on the left again continue through a metal gate, skirt the remains of a pool, cross a stile and head for a wooden gate. Veer left to a gate to the road.

Turn right at the road and in a short distance go through a gate on the left, just past a tin barn. Carry straight on, with the hedge on the right, to two gates (together), one metal, one wooden. Immediately turn right under a wire and climb a stile. (The OS map shows the path on the original side of the hedge but there is no stile at the proper crossing point.) Turn left and with the hedge on the left go over a stile at the next hedge. Turn right and follow the wire fence on the right to a metal gate and road. Turn right onto the road to a metal gate just before a bungalow (**C**). (*The shorter walk joins here*)

There are several ploughed fields on the next path and it may be hard to follow when the crops are fully grown unless the route is reinstated. The path should go diagonally across the field but there is no way out in the corner, so keep right of diagonal and aim for a metal gate. Continue in the same general direction to the next metal gate with a pool on the left; then keep straight ahead, aiming for Madam's Hill and a broken wooden gate with a dried-up pool on the right.

Follow the hedge on the left to an opening halfway along and, once through it, turn right over a wire fence. Keeping the hedge on the right, still aim for the hill when the hedge ends. Go through a gap with a dried pool on the right and keep straight ahead, first to a metal gate, then to a wooden fence. Veer left to a stile in the hedge and follow the boundary around Broughton Court, a sixteenth-century half-timbered house, though much altered over the years. (If you look to the left there is a fine view across to Hanbury Church.)

After passing the Court veer left to a stile in the hedge and to a lane. Turn left and at the junction left again; and, shortly, turn right into a field and climb a metal fence between two wooden gates by a conifer plantation. To the right, nestling under Madam's Hill, is Mere Hall, regarded as one of Worcestershire's most impressive timber-framed buildings. Part of its middle section may be as early as the fourteenth century though much of the house was built in the seventeenth century and some alterations are very recent. The Bearcroft family is said to have owned the estate from the fourteenth to twentieth centuries.

Follow a hedge on the right and go through a wooden gate. Cross over the drive to Mere Hall and go through another wooden gate. Turn left and walk carefully through a newly planted wood; then keep ahead to the footbridge noted at the beginning of the walk (ignoring the footbridge on the right). Continue straight across the field to the stile and the starting point.

Madam's Hill

Walk 11
9½ miles *or* 5 miles
Bromsgrove Station — Droitwich Station

Waterways, railways and traditional pubs

OS Pathfinder Map	974 (SO 86/96)
Start	Bromsgrove Staton (GR 969693)
Finish	Droitwich Station (GR 893633)

This is one of the two non-circular walks in the book. Since it starts in Bromsgrove and ends in Droitwich, it means *either* returning to Bromsgrove by train or bus (the 144) *or* parking in Droitwich, travelling by public transport to Bromsgrove, then following the walk. Of course you could just try to persuade someone to meet you at Droitwich.

The route crosses three different railway lines, meets up with two different canals and goes under a motorway, reminding us of the engineering prowess of man. But for all that this walk is mostly farming country and there are at least seven pubs on the way — most of them traditonal, most of them named.

From the station walk up to the *Dragoon Hotel*, turn right past the car park and butcher and right again down St Godwald's Road and back over the railway line. In railway history this is a famous spot — the Lickey Incline starts here, the railway hill that rises almost an inch for every yard of its 2¼-mile stretch to Blackwell. It remains the steepest bank on any British main line and when steam ruled only with the aid of a couple of banking engines - or the giant Big Bertha - could a train make it up the slope. To the right is the site of the old Railway Carriage and Wagon Works — now a housing estate. One of the roads is appropriately named after the Birmingham and Gloucester's chief engineer, James McConnell, whose house stood beside this bridge's predecessor. He designed the saddletank engine and was instrumental in founding the Institution of Mechanical Engineers.

Continue down the lane past the cricket and tennis clubs; and where the road goes sharp left turn right along Lower Gambold's Lane past Maidsmere Cottage. Carry straight on through a gate, a field and a second gate; then turn left up a hill to a stile and bear slightly left up to another stile by a gate on the brow of a hill. In the next two fields keep to the right of the hedge down to the canal and cross by the footbridge to the right of the lock. Turn right onto the towpath (**A**).

The climb from the Severn Vale to the Midland plateau presented problems for the canal builders as well as the railway men and the Worcester — Birmingham Canal was not quite built overnight. Exactly 200 years ago the Bill giving it the go-ahead was passed and there was much rejoicing — bells were rung, songs were sung, poems were penned.

START

FINISH

53

But not everywhere: the oppostition had spent twice as much — £20,000 — and their only consolation must have been to watch the difficulties facing the engineers. Between Worcester and Tardebigge 58 locks were needed to raise the level and the Tardebigge flight of 30 locks remains the longest flight of narrow locks in the country. By 1807 the canal had got as far as Tardebigge; it was 1815 before it reached Worcester. (For a glimpse of what this stretch was like when it was a *working* canal see Alan White's article in *The Rousler No. 1*, published by The Bromsgrove Society; and Pat Warner's book, *Lock Keeper's Daughter*)

Follow the towpath for 1¼ miles, passing the *Queen's Head* and leave the canal at lock 23 by the boatyard. *If preferred,* stay on the towpath for about another mile and join the walk at point **B**. At the road turn left (the *Navigation Inn* is just up to the right) and walk past L G Harris & Co to a footpath on the right just before the end of the woods around the industrial park. After 100 yards climb a stile on the left, then cross the field to a stile by the electricity pylon. Turn left and follow the hedge to the top of the rise; then bear left through a gate and keep along the right of the hedge, passing Weston Hall Farm on the right and reaching a stile in the hedge on the left by a redbrick house.

Cross the field, bearing right to a signpost in the lane near New Elms Farm — but *don't* take the signposted footpath opposite. Instead, turn right and after 200 yards follow the sign which points obliquely left at a field gate. Follow the angle across the field to a gate just past the tree; and then continue in the same direction across the next field to a stile near some trees. Over this stile keep left along the edge to a lane and turn right.

Cross the canal at bridge no. 41 and continue to the T-junction. (To the left — about 200 yards — is the *Bowling Green Inn*). Turn right towards Stoke Works — and the *Boat and Railway Inn* and the *Butcher's Arms!* — and after 100 yards turn left to cross a railway footbridge (over the Birmingham — Bristol line). Keep left of the hedge for about 200 yards, then continue on the righthand side to cross a second railway footbridge (over the line which goes through Droitwich and on to Worcester).

To the left here — in a straight line across the fields — is Wychbold Church, in style fourteenth-century, in reality just over 100 hundred years old, built at the expense of John Corbett, the 'salt king'. The most striking feature is its floor. Walk the length of its interior and you begin to think you are on board ship.

About 25 yards from the footbridge climb a 'stile' on the right and head across the field towards Sagebury Farm and to a stile to the right of a gate in line with the barn. Turn left alongside the outbuildings, then bear right down a slope passing two gates on the left to a narrow strip with, on the right, Upton Warren's best-known feature, the nature reserve managed by the Worcestershire Nature Conservation Trust.

Keep straight on, passing the BBC's Droitwich transmitter on the left, then the support wires of a smaller pylon; and aim towards the houses ahead. Walk along the left of a drive to a stile onto the A38 (**C**). Cross the main road *taking great care*, then walk towards Droitwich for a short distance. Just past a row of three cottages turn into a drive that leads to Little Gains Farm. Go through the gate and over the River Salwarpe; climb a fence on the left by an electricity pole and then bear right 45° towards the sheep pens in the corner of the field, 100 yards to the left of Little Gains Farm, crossing the intervening fence at a convenient point.

Go through the pens to a stile and then turn left to a fence with a cross-step and follow a hedge on the left to a stile into a small rough area. With the Salwarpe on the left cross a track and then climb a stile into a field between the motorway (M5) and the river. Keep straight on in this field to a stile into another field, pass a footbridge on the left and follow the river to a gate into Crown Lane. 200 yards to the left is *The Crown* and the bus if you feel you have walked far enough.

Turn right under the motorway bridge, then recross the Salwarpe at a footbridge on the left opposite a road junction. Cross the field alongside the M5 to a stile and then continue on to a field just before Walkmills Farm. Turn right to a stile in the corner of a field, then right between two pools. Cross a footbridge back over the Salwarpe to a stile and then bear 45° left across a field to a hedge on the right.

Follow the hedge to a stile, turn right and then cross the next field, with a cottage on the right, to a stile near some corrugated steel sheds. Do not cross this stile but instead turn left through a farm gate and follow a bridleway through a small gate and on to where the hedge on the right ends. Turn right down to Salty Brook, then go up the track to the road by the whitewashed Ford Cottages (**D**).

Cross the road to a bridleway almost opposite (waymarked with the crown of the Wychavon Way) and continue up the slope past a metal gate to another gate. Follow the track, which can be very muddy in wet weather, with the wooded slope on the right to a gate at the end. Bear right down a field to a tree and a water trough; then here bear sharp left and climb over the brow of a hill to a stile by a tree in the corner of the field. Over the stile turn right: ahead you can see Driotwich. Keep the hedge on the right to the fence into the woods around the wonderfully named Highstank Pool and then follow the indistinct track with the pool on the left to the far end of the woods.

Go to the right of the hedge ahead and follow it to a stile in the corner of the field. Over the stile the map shows the footpath continuing across the field; but it may be easier to follow the farm track going alongside the railway, turning left to the corner of the field by the edge of a golf course. At this point head straight across the next field, making for a tree in the fence in line with the tower of Dodderhill Church in the distance. At the tree, where the remains of an old kissing gate lie rusting away, cross the fence and follow a fence on the right. Then bear left to cross the fence and go under the Droitwich bypass. Follow this line past the remains of a fence to a line of trees ahead. Turn left and then right at a gate across the railway line (which runs on to Kidderminster and Wolverhampton) and down the tracks to Vines Lane. Turn left to the *Gardener's Arms* and then go right, through the houses, to a footbridge over the River Salwarpe.

Over the footbridge turn right and follow the line of the river with the Droitwich Canal on the left. The canal, built by James Brindley to enable salt to be carried down to the Severn and on to Bristol, was left derelict half a century ago. But in recent years it has been dredged and weeded, much of the towpath cleaned up and new lock gates made. Where the canal opens into a basin bear right and follow the footpath onto the road near the *Railway Hotel*. Cross the road and then bear right to the canal towpath under the railway bridges. Carry on along the towpath to the next bridge under the new road, and as you emerge turn right up the steps. Do not cross the road but turn right, crossing the canal on the footway. Then turn right and back down the steps to the canal; go back under the road and take the tarmac path bearing right past the British Legion Club and up the slope to the railway station.

Worcester — Birmingham Canal

Walk 12   *On and off the Clents*

9 miles
Clent — Hagley — Broome — Clent
OS Pathfinder Maps   953 (SO 87/97) & 933 (SO 88/98)
Start and finish   Layby on the wooded side of the A491 between the
Clent turning and the *Holly Bush Inn* (GR 929781)

The Clent Hills, part of the ridge stretching from Kinver Edge to the
Lickeys, rise to over 1000 feet and are dominated by Walton Hill in the
east and Adam's Hill in the west. A lot of the area is open grassland and
there are wonderful panoramic views from the rounded gorse-covered
tops. But there are densely wooded areas too and some fairly boggy
valleys — so be prepared for all types of walking.

The hilly parish of Clent belonged to Staffordshire for several
hundred years before being returned to Worcestershire in the last
century. Tradition has it that the ancient Britons fought a battle in this
area, camping on the eve on these hills; that the kings of Mercia had a
residence here; and that Kenelm, eight-year old son of King Kenulf of
Mercia, was killed by the lover of his jealous sister and buried in the
woods under a thorn tree. The body was miraculously discovered
through the appearance of a dove at Rome which carried a scroll giving
details of the death. A fountain burst forth at the place where the body
was found and formed a stream which was considered to bring good
health to all who drank it.

From the layby walk towards Hagley for about 100 yards. Climb
the stile at the signposted footpath and walk straight ahead across the
field. Then, with a hedge on the left, continue to a stile in the corner of
the field, turn left onto a bridleway and at the T-junction take the footpath
opposite, slightly to the right. Bear left across a field to a gate and
continue in the same direction across the next field passing some farm
buildings on the left. Climb the fence/stile, cross the lane and go over
another stile. With the hedge on the right head towards a stile in the
corner of the field , join a driveway and turn left. At the end of the drive
go through a metal wicket gate opposite and make diagonally across the
field for some white gates.

Turn right into Walton Pool Lane and walk along to Clent village.
The church, on the right, both leans and slopes (despite extensive
rebuilding in 1865), the chancel several feet higher than the rest of the
building. Pass the church and cross the road, taking the drive to the left
of a row of cottages. This leads to a footpath between hedgerows and,
later, with a metal fence on the right. Continue past a very steep track
on the left (this is the one for the young and energetic!) and turn left

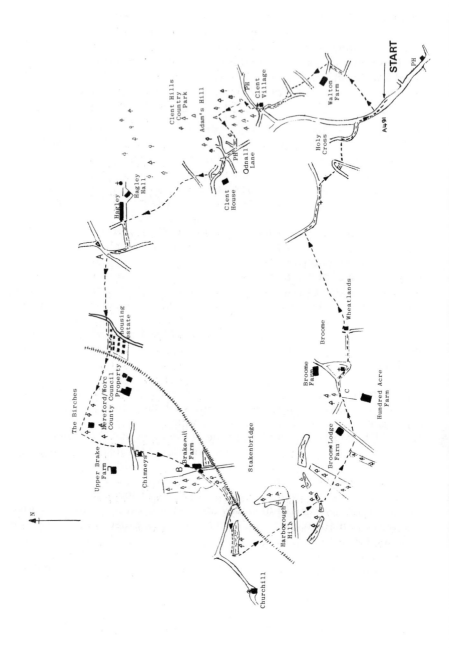

START

PH

A491

Walton
Farm

Holy
Cross

Clent
Village

PH

Clent Hills
Country
Park

Adam's Hill

PH

Odnall
Lane

Clent
House

Hagley

Hagley
Hall

A

Housing
Estate

The Birches

Hereford/Worc
County Council
Property

Upper Brake
Farm

Chimneys

Brakemill
Farm

B

Stakenbridge

Harborough
Hill

Churchill

Broome Lodge
Farm

Hundred Acre
Farm

C

Broome
Farm

Broome

Wheatlands

N

58

the path forks left again at the junction of footpaths.

A breather can be taken here and there's an ideally situated seat for the purpose. Pass on the left the steep track mentioned above — the path keeps to the woodside with a fence on the left. At the junction of four paths go straight ahead, climbing a number of steps to Adam's Hill. Proceed to the top of the hill for another rest, splendid views and the four standing stones which, despite their looks, are not a bit ancient but put there by Lord Lyttleton in the eighteenth century to 'improve' the look of the place.

Now return to the junction of broad paths (passed after the steps up to the hill) and head towards a group of Scots pines, leaving the main track, which leads to the *Fountain Inn*, and continuing straight ahead, passing a white house on the right to join a narrow lane. At the T-junction turn right into Odnall Lane and walk past the *Fountain Inn* . Continue across the drive, a high brick wall on the right, to the Sunfield Children's Home and shortly after take the footpath on the right signposted to Hagley.

Cross the drive to Clent Grove and with hedgerows on either side arrive at a stile. The walk now joins a section of the North Worcestershire Path (**see** Walk 14 for a note about this long-distance path). With wire fences on both sides go through a metal wicket gate and on reaching a road turn left. (A little further along to the right is the entrance to Hagley Hall, a mid-eighteenth-century Palladian-style building which has been the seat of the Lyttleton family for over four centuries. It was here that the last of the Gunpowder Plot conspirators, Stephen Lyttleton and Robert Wyntour were finally caught after hiding out in various parts of Worcestershire and Staffordshire — **see** Walk 9.) Along the road turn right at the T-junction, cross the dual carriageway at the car showrooms and take the footpath opposite to Worcester Lane (**A**).

Continue along the well used and waymarked path, cross a road and rejoin the path which runs between wooden fences and leads to a small housing estate. Walk through the estate, ignoring all roads to the right and left. At a cul-de-sac the path again runs between high wooden fences for a short distance. Cross a small bridge over a culvert and then over the railway line and continue, with the hedge on the right, through Hereford and Worcester County Council property. Climb a stile and, proceeding with the hedge on the left, turn left at the third stile (waymarked North Worcestershire Path). At the lane turn right for about 20 yards, then left at the signposted path to the left of a large house (Chimneys).

With hedges on both sides carry straight ahead, over a stile, through a gate and onto a lane with farm buildings on the left. Almost immediately take a tarmac track on the right with Brakesmill Farmhouse on the left (**B**). A short walk to the lake in this peaceful little hamlet may be rewarded by the sight of one or even more herons.

After some 70 yards leave the tarmac and continue straight ahead through a wood; then, with a lake on the left, join the road. Turn right, take care crossing the road and after a short distance take a footpath on the left towards Churchill. On a well marked path and with another lake on the left continue to a rough-surfaced lane. Turn left and walk along the head of the lake to a metal gate ahead. (In the eighteenth century this area abounded in damsons and plums, enough to supply all the neighbouring markets; and the lords of the manor, the Dickenses, are said to be ancestors of the great Charles.) Carry straight ahead and cross a field, keeping to the right of the third tree in a line of oaks. Cross the railway line (but don't forget to stop, look and listen first).

Keeping straight ahead, make for the left of the fourth in a line of four tall trees. Go through a gap in the hedge and on reaching the road turn left. After about 20 yards cross the road to join a signposted footpath, then bear slightly left across a field to a wood and the corner of a fenced area. Pass a 'No fishing' sign, go between two small pools — often dry — and through a metal gate; and follow the hedge on the right for a short distance. Where the hedge makes a 90° right turn, head straight across the field to the woodland opposite. Go through a gap in the hedge and climb the hillside on a broad and well used path. Continue to the road.

Cross over and take a signposted path which, on a 45° line, heads for the lefthand corner of the field. The fifth telegraph pole from the farm, which can be seen against the trees in front, is a useful guide (**C**). Cross a stile and ditch, then turn right to Broome village. Broome (which seems, incidentally, to have aquired its 'e' in the last few decades) stands in the middle of the hilly parish, beautifully set to the west of the Clent Hills, tucked away from the main roads. Until the late eighteenth century broom flourished on open common land here but it is difficult to know whether the Worcestershire writer John Noake was jubilant or depressed when he wrote in 1868 that Broome had

> *No manufactures or public works, no local*
> *squire, no mansion, no Dissenters' chapel, no*
> *church-rate disturbances, no Fenianism or*
> *agitation of any sort.*

It's a sign of the times that whereas fifty years ago the area was largely agricultural now many farms have disappeared and the farmhouses are lived in by non-farmers.

Take the right fork, passing the tiny Georgian brick-built church of St Peter on the left, and continue straight ahead to a bridleway signposted 'No through road'. Turn left at the T-junction, pass a pair of cottages on the right and continue first between hedgerows and then with the hedge on the left to join a lane. Turn right towards Holy Cross and at a group of cottages turn right down a narrow lane to join a footpath signposted 'No horse riding' alongside the village play area on the right. Carry on through the allotments to the road. Cross this and Holy Cross Lane ahead and take the footpath to the left of a bungalow. Turn right on reaching the road (Bromsgrove Road), then right again where the road joins the bypass. A couple of hundred yards along cross back to the starting point.

Walk 13   *In the valley of the Arrow*
8½ miles
Studley — Coughton — Studley
OS Pathfinder Maps 975 (SP 06/16) & 997 (SP 05/15)
                    (Only a tiny section of the latter is needed — it
                    could easily be done without.)
Start and finish Car park behind the library and village hall
                      (GR 071636)

We have cheated a little by including this walk — we know it's not in
Worcestershire! But it's a very pleasant area to walk in and both Studley
and Coughton have long had connections with Worcestershire.
    The first part of the route is very much a riverside walk, following
for most of the way the River Arrow which flows south-east out of
Redditch to skirt the eastern edge of Studley and wind through Spernall
and Coughton before joining the Avon. The second half of the walk leaves
the river behind and crosses more undulating countryside, following the
edge of several bits of woodland.

    Leave the car park by the pedestrian exit in the north corner near
the school, signposted to Alcester Road. Cross the A435, which is the
old Roman road, and walk down Castle Road. Take the first right
(Gunner's Lane) to the end and then turn left down a fenced path to a stile
in the fence on the right. Over the stile follow the River Arrow on the left
as far as the footbridge, cross and then immediately turn right. With the
river now on the right head straight on for a stile and then on to a metal
gate.
    Turn left and follow the hedge to a footbridge over a stream which
feeds the Arrow, cross over and go on to another stile. Then follow the
hedge on the right to a metal gate. Once through the gate pass to the right
of the farm buildings (Spernall Hall Farm), threading your way between
various bits of machinery to a metalled track. Follow the track through
three gates to the road, turn left and immediately right along the lane.
    There's not a lot to Spernall, this very rural community comprising
for the most part scattered farms of orange brick, some early nineteenth-
century cottages, a Georgian rectory and a derelict stone-and-brick
church. But from this peaceful spot there is a lovely wide view south
along the river valley.
    Just past the church go through a wicket gate to the right and
cross the field, heading for the oak tree just to the right of the farmhouse;
and make for the stile ahead (*ignoring* the more obvious footbridge over
the Arrow on the right). There are now four fields to cross and they are
usually cultivated. Head first for a metal gate facing you, then carry on

62

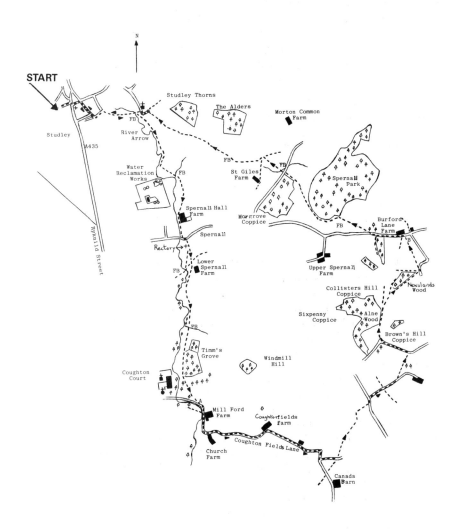

N

START

Studley Thorns

The Alders

Morton Common
Farm

FB

Studley

River
Arrow

A435

Water
Reclamation
Works

FB

FB

St Giles
Farm

FB

Spernall
Park

Ryknild Street

Spernall Hall
Farm

Morgrove
Coppice

FB

Burford
Lane
Farm

Spernall

Rectory

Upper Spernall
Farm

Collisters Hill
Coppice

Newslands
Wood

Lower
Spernall
Farm

FB

Sixpenny
Coppice

Alne
Wood

Brown's Hill
Coppice

FB

Timm's
Grove

Windmill
Hill

Coughton
Court

A

Mill Ford
Farm

Coughtonfields
Farm

Coughton Fields Lane

Church
Farm

Canada
Barn

63

to a gap in a wooden fence. In the same direction, make for a gate and footbridge and finally carry straight on to a wooden gate leading to a grassy field.

Follow the line of oak trees on the left and then bear left to a gate in the corner. From this field, to the right, are views of Coughton Court and some, at least, will have decided from the outset to allow time to visit this very interesting house. It was built in the early sixteenth century and for five-and-a-half centuries was the seat of one of the West Midlands' leading Catholic families, the Throckmortons, who moved here from Worcestershire when they inherited the estate.

Like other Catholics they had no easy ride. In 1583 they led the plot to murder Elizabeth I and put Mary Queen of Scots in her place; in 1605 they were indirectly involved in the Gunpowder Plot; in the Civil War Coughton was occupied by Parliamentarians and bombarded by Royalists, the house itself sacked and set on fire; and in 1688 the east wing was destroyed — and never rebuilt — by a Protestant mob from Alcester. In 1945 the Court became the property of the National Trust but the contents, including some fine paintings and Jacobean relics, remain in the possession of the family. In the saloon may be seen the staircase that was once in Harvington Hall before it — and a variety of furnishings — were stripped away and brought here (**see** Walk 1).

Once through the gate in the corner of the field head towards two tree stumps close to the hedge on the right; then look for a stile down the bank that leads into Coughton Lane(**A**). Turn left and follow the lane for about 1¼ miles until just after a sharp righthand bend where you leave the road and enter a tree-lined bridleway on the left. Climb up as far as an opening on the left waymarked Heart of England Way — opposite a pond.

Follow the clearly defined path, first through a young oak plantation and then with the hedge on the right to a gap between two trees and a waymarked footbridge. Carry on to another footbridge and stile to pass the cottage on the right into the lane. Turn left and then immediately right and follow the track (waymarked) to a stile in the fence on the left. Climb the slope to a stile by a metal gate and continue with the hedge on the right to a stile into the road.

Turn left along the road to where at a sharp lefthand bend a rising farm track leaves on the right via a cattle-grid and metal gate. Just past some farm buildings on the left go through a waymarked gate on the left and follow the track to another gate; and then continue with the woods on the left. As the woods end go ahead to a stile on a bank to the left of a waymarked gate and cross a field to a metal gate and the road (**B**).

Turn left and 200 yards past a thatched cottage — as you descend a steep hill — climb a bank on the right to a stile. Over the stile, turn diagonally left (heading for the lefthand edge of Spernall Park in the distance) and cross the field in the same direction to a stile. Carry on to a gate and footbridge at the edge of the park, then follow the edge to a farm track, turning left, then right as you skirt the wood.

Where the track enters the wood take the left waymarked fork and follow the hedge on the left over a footbridge and stile past the wood on the left (Morgrove Coppice) to the road. Cross the road and waymarked fence opposite, climb the bank and then walk diagonally left to the footbridge and stile ahead. With the hedge and brook on the left go on to a metal gate, pass through and then with the hedge and brook now on the right carry on to a metal gate onto a farm track.

Bear left with the track to where it turns right. Here, go through a large gap in the hedge and head towards the lefthand side of the trees on the brow of the hill. From here Studley Church can be seen: head straight for it, following the hedge on the left to Church Lane. Turn left and go to a wooden kissing gate on the left opposite the church.

Most of Studley lies to the west of the A435; but it is on this north-eastern side, nearer to the river, that evidence of its early settlement is to be found. The church is quite striking, with its perpendicular tower, Norman herringbone masonry, sandstone chancel and red-tiled roof; and just north of the church is the site on which firstly a castle was built, soon after the Norman Conquest, and then much later, in the sixteenth century, a partly timber-framed house.

Cross the field to the footbridge crossed at the start of the walk and retrace the route to the car park.

Walk 14   *Up hill and down dale*

8 miles

Bittell Reservoirs — Wast Hill — Forhill — Bittell Reservoirs

OS Pathfinder Map   954 (SP 07/17)

Start and finish   Roadside verge ¼ mile along the road to Lower Bittell Reservoir from the B4120 (GR 016744)

A walk whose northern point touches the edge of England's second city — and you wouldn't know it. The Cofton Hackett area was for most of its history largely agricultural but in the last century a number of nailmakers worked here. Now it is a mainly residential area, the broad-leaved woods of the Lickey Hills given or purchased to provide open space for Brummies.

The eastern part of this undulating walk is in places remarkably unspoilt. There's a hint of the Derbyshire moors about it which would be even stronger if the low hedges were to be replaced by dry-stone walls. But as well as its varying natural beauty the walk contains three excellent examples of man's engineering genius: the Bittell Reservoirs, the Wasthill Tunnel and the Roman Road, Ryknild Street.

At the bend, where the road goes over the causeway across Lower Bittell Reservoir, take the wooded bridleway alongside the lake following the stream from the upper reservoir. Lower Bittell Reservoir was built to maintain water supplies to mill owners on the River Arrow (like those at Alvechurch, for example) while Upper Bittell Reservoir was built in 1832 to feed the Worcester — Birmingham Canal; and to the right can be seen the remains of the old pumping house.

There is a view of the English Civil War that the only vandals were Cromwell and his men. Proof that Royalists were not averse to destroying some fine buildings in the name of war lies on the other side of the railway line. On 14 May 1645 Charles I, having set fire to Hawkesley Hall on Clent Ridge, arrived at Cofton Hall, stayed the night and promptly set fire to that before leaving for Chester. Fortunately, some fine fourteenth-century work remains.

Carry on past the ponds on the left to where the road turns sharp left. Take the footpath on the right and with the hedge on the left follow the path round to the barns. Continue on around the field to the stile in the corner. Cross the next field to a gate and then follow the hedge on the right to the next gate at the bottom of the slope.

Cross the next field diagonally up the slope to a stile. Over this, follow the path along the hedge on the right until it reaches the road (Longbridge Lane). Cross this lane and walk towards the A441 Birmingham to Alvechurch road and cross *with great care,* using the

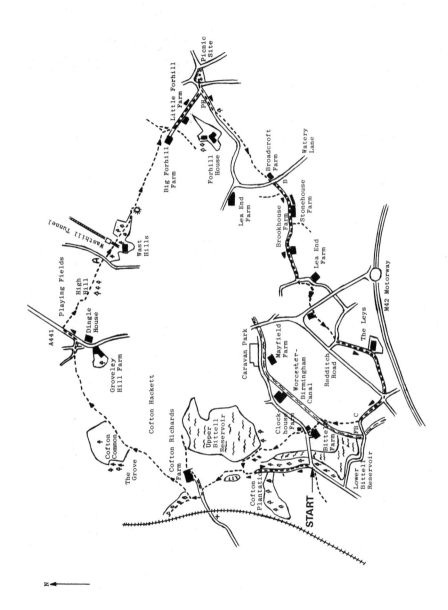

N ←

START

67

traffic islands. Walk along the grass verge on the A441 towards Birmingham for about 200 yards until a stile and sign are reached. Turn right and you are now on the North Worcestershire Path which stretches 21 miles from Kingsford Country Park (on the edge of Kinver) to Forhill Picnic Site, the most easterly point on this walk. The path is maintained by the county's Countryside Service and clearly-marked yellow arrows should prevent even inexperienced walkers from getting lost or straying onto private land.

Follow the path up the hill, past the small copse and then between the fence and the hedge by Wast Hills Playing Fields. Bear left at the buildings and then right to reach Wasthill Lane (**A**). Turn right and then take the path on the left by the side of the trees up the slope to a track. You have just walked over Wasthill Tunnel, built in 1796. Of the five tunnels along the Worcester — Birmingham Canal Wasthill is by far the longest at nearly 3000 yards. In the early years boats were legged through the tunnel and the horses led across the top (vividly described in Eileen W Davies' recent book *Seechem Chronicles*). Later, tugs were used to tow the boats through.

Take the track ahead until it bears left and cross the stile on the right. Follow the hedge on the left until you cross another track. Cross the field ahead and after passing rough ground to the right take the stile in the hedge on the right which leads to a farm track. Turn left and follow the track to the *Peacock Inn* and Forhill Picnic Site. It's an excellent half-way resting point with eating, picnic and toilet facilities; and those of a philosophical turn of mind can muse on the straightness of the Roman road which separates the pub from the picnic site. On the map it is Ryknild Street, on the signpost Icknield Street, either way the name in all likelihood borrowed from the famous ancient British way which runs from Norfolk to Dorset.

When you're rearing to go again, take the lane passing the pub on the left and follow it downhill to a stile on the left in a small wood. Follow this path through the wood to another stile; and in the fields ahead follow the hedge on the right through a gate and onto a stile in the hedge ahead. Follow the hedge, now on the left, down to Broadcroft Farm, emerging opposite a T-junction (**B**).

Take the road ahead past Stonehouse Farm on the left and at the next T-junction take the path ahead into the cricket ground. Bear round to the left past the pavilion and then leave the ground over a footbridge in the hedge, cross another field and then cross the new M42 link road. Cross the field ahead with the buildings and pond on the right, go over the stile into the garden and then turn right out of the garden into the track and left across the field, leaving it via the stile into the garden of the last cottage in the block.

Passing via the front garden, go right to a T-junction with a grassy island in the centre. Take the lane on the left at the triangle and walk ⅓ mile to the island on the A441. Cross the main road and take the footpath by the side of the Barnt Green road as far as a signposted stile on the right where the road goes sharp left towards the canal bridge (**C**). This stile leads via a short track to a small bridge from where the path runs diagonally across the field to the canal bridge.

Cross the bridge and carry on towards Bittell Farm. Go through the gates and then right through the next gate, emerging into the lane. Cross the lane to a stile and follow the track along the hedge on the right to a stile leading into the pleasant grounds of the Bittell Reservoirs. Follow the embankment to the buildings where the track on the left leads past the ruined pumphouse to the original lane. Turn left and back to the starting point.

Upper Bittell Reservoir

Walk 15   *Fields and woods*
                                                          around Dodford

3 miles and 5 miles
Battlefield Farm — Dodford — Battlefield Farm
OS Pathfinder Map   953 (SO 87/97)
Start and finish   Layby on the north side of the A448, 1¼ miles
                    from Bromsgrove (GR 939713)

A walk around the parish of Dodford with Grafton, passing through a village with a very distinctive history before taking to the woods that were once part of the enlarged Forest of Feckenham.

From the layby walk towards Kidderminster for about 200 yards to a stile and signpost on the right. Enter the field here and follow the hedge on the left downhill, over a stile and across another field to a fence/stile. In the next field cross the bridge and then bear slightly right to a ditch-and-stile crossing in the corner. From here the footpath goes diagonally across and uphill to the corner of the hedges on the right. Follow the hedge on the right to the stile in the corner.

Over the stile the path follows the line of trees straight across (with Fockbury Farm and the barn conversions over to the left) to the holly hedge. From the stile by the gate cross the next field, heading slightly right and downhill to the side of the barns by Spout House on the right. Cross the lane into a narrow field and with the hedge on the left make for the fence at the end. Over the fence, follow the hedge right to another stile at a footpath junction; then turn left uphill with the hedge on the left.

This little part of the world is Housman country. Bromsgrove's most famous son was born in 1859 at Valley House (now renamed Housmans) but moved when he was only a few months old to Perry Hall. He was back here when he was thirteen, however, for his father decided to move his by then large family to Fockbury House (usually known as The Clock House), almost all of it demolished in the 1960s.

At the point where the path crosses to the other side of the hedge turn round for a wonderful panoramic view of Bromsgrove with Tardebigge Church in silhouette on the skyline. Then follow the path to the road opposite the cottages at Alfred's Well (nothing to do with Alfred of burnt cookies fame, much more to do with the family called Orford who owned the land from the sixteenth century). At the road go left to the signpost — yes, it does point to Dodford in two different directions, just to underline how scattered the village is!

Turn right down the hill for ¼ mile to Alfred's Well House and immediately after the house turn right up a leafy track through Sunnyhill Coppice, emerging at a field. Follow the hedge on the right to a stile, cross

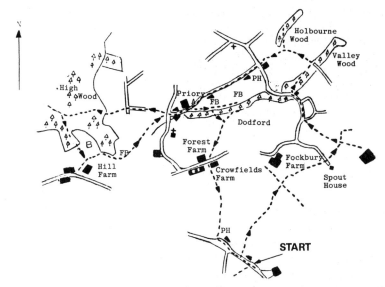

Holbourne
Wood

Valley
Wood

PH

High
Wood

Priory
FB
FB

Dodford

Forest
Farm

Hill
Farm

Crowfields
Farm

Fockbury
Farm

Spout
House

PH

START

over and drop down the bank. Immediately turn left, cross a stile and follow the hedge on the left to a gate about 50 yards before Holbourne Wood. Go through the gate and bear right down the slope to where another gate opens onto a muddy track. Cross the bridge into a field and bear left uphill past the gardens to a stile into a narrow path which leads to the road opposite Whinfield Road.

Walk along Whinfield Road past the *Dodford Inn* and downhill to the end of the lane; then branch off into the bridleway on the left near the gateway to the The Poplars (a large modern house). The bridleway comes out onto the concrete drive of Rose Lane (**A**).

For the short walk the return journey starts here. See below for directions.

For the longer walk carry on along Rose Lane and cross the bridge to the road at the bottom of the hill (Rose Hill) with Dodford Church on the left and Dodford Priory ¼ mile to the right. Both, if there is time, are worth walking to; but the presencce of a double hedge will prevent any view of the Priory except in the leafless part of the year. It was founded some 800 years ago and dissolved in 1538. What remained of that building was incorporated into a handsome Tudor house, lived in by the Fownes family for more than a century and a half. In the other direction the church's history is quite different: it was erected in 1908, replacing an earlier building which stood on the site of today's village hall, and appropriately its special quality comes from the Art Nouveau wood and plasterwork carried out by members of the Bromsgrove Guild which

71

achieved worldwide fame in the earlier years of this century.

To see Dodford'a particular claim to fame you will need to walk on beyond the Priory to the heart of the former Chartist settlement, established in the late 1840s by Feargus O'Connor. It was not the most successful bit of planning but the Chartist cottages were homes of quality and a number have survived.

Cross the main road (Priory Road) to the stile to the right of the cottage and follow the path beside the fence through the field of anthills. (These and the woods attract woodpeckers to the area.) At the end of the fence cross a stile into a narrow track that rises up to the end of a lane. Follow the lane to the sharp righthand bend and at this point go through the gate ahead into the field and down to the footbridge. Cross the footbridge and a stile into High Wood and follow the track ahead for about ½ mile.

Look carefully for a cross-track by a beech tree on the left and turn left, following the track at first downhill and then uphill to the edge of the wood and onto the hill (**B**) from which there are excellent views of Bredon Hill, the Malverns and the Abberley Hills, with the Welsh hills beyond them. Go down to the stile in the corner between the wood and the hedge ahead, follow the edge of the wood to another stile and then the hedge on the left to a bridge and gate.

Through the gate head diagonally uphill across the field to a stile in the corner leading into another field of anthills and the stile in the fence passed earlier on. Turn right, cross back to Rose Lane and walk to the point where the bridleway leaves the concrete. *This is the point where the shorter walk begins the return* (**A**).

Cross the field to the right of the bridleway to a stile, then follow the path across the next field until just before the hedge where a track on the right leads down to a footbridge. At the top of the opposite bank climb a double stile, and then cross the field to another double stile. Turn right here and follow the hedge to an awkward stile next to a gate. Cross the next field diagonally to a stile by the side of the barn at Forest Farm, then cross the road (Fockbury Road) to the signposted footpath — the sign was broken in early 1991 — by the side of Crowfield Farm Stables.

Follow the path, with the hedge on the left, over three stiles, emerging via concrete steps onto the car park of the *Park Gate Inn*. Follow the old road left back to the main road and then to the layby, passing on the way Battlefield Farm, named not after a skirmish in the Civil War but a battle much earlier — though which one, precisely, it is impossible now to say. Certainly this bit of land was already called Battlefield by the beginning of the sixteenth century.